THE RELATION OF THE JUDICIARY TO THE CONSTITUTION

Da Capo Press Reprints in

AMERICAN CONSTITUTIONAL AND LEGAL HISTORY

GENERAL EDITOR: LEONARD W. LEVY

Claremont Graduate School

THE RELATION
OF THE JUDICIARY
TO THE CONSTITUTION

By William M. Meigs

DA CAPO PRESS • NEW YORK • 1971

A Da Capo Press Reprint Edition

This Da Capo Press edition of
The Relation of the Judiciary to the Constitution
is an unabridged republication of the first
edition published in New York in 1919.

Library of Congress Catalog Card Number 73-124896
SBN 306-71988-6

Published by Da Capo Press, Inc.
A Subsidiary of Plenum Publishing Corporation
227 West 17th Street, New York, N.Y. 10011

Manufactured in the United States of America

THE RELATION OF THE JUDICIARY
TO THE CONSTITUTION

The
Relation of the Judiciary to the Constitution

BY

WILLIAM M. MEIGS

Author of "The Life of John C. Calhoun," "The Life of Thomas H.
Benton," "The Life of Charles Jared Ingersoll," "The Growth
of the Constitution," and Other Works

THE NEALE PUBLISHING COMPANY
440 FOURTH AVENUE, NEW YORK
MCMXIX

TABLE OF CONTENTS

TABLE OF CONTENTS

INTRODUCTION

THE subject of the present book has for many years been of interest to the writer. Long ago, while still a young lawyer, I was in some way drawn to a study of the judiciary in relation to the Constitution; and under the same title as that which now, late in life, I am placing upon this book, I wrote the second of a series of law articles, to the writing of which ill-health and a dearth of practice had directed me.

I may without vanity say that, prior to the publication of the article in question in 1885,[1] there was but the most insufficient treatment of the subject to be found. Kent's pages, and those of Story, Cooley, and the other writers, would have been searched in vain for any valid sketch of its history, either in the Federal Convention or in the early cases in which it was applied or hinted at.

As my studies preparatory to the article went on at the time in question, I was surprised at the number of cases in point which I found; but it must not be supposed that these were easily unearthed from the dust of a century. The indices to the old and oddly printed reports of that long-ago day were of no assistance. There was, then, never, or rarely, an index-heading of

[1] *American Law Review* (March-April, 1885), Vol. XIX, pp. 175-203.

"Constitution," or "Constitutional," or any such ready
road by which to find the cases I sought; and decisions
that the veriest tyro of an index-maker would to-day
refer to some such easy pigeon-hole, were then sure to
be found somewhere adrift under "Ejectment," "Dis-
seizin," or perhaps "Jury." The only possible way to
find them was to go carefully over every item of the
"Index," with the aid, too, of frequent reference to the
text of the book in hand. I well remember so toiling
through the volumes,—not very many,—of law reports
of our pre- and early Constitutional period in all the
old thirteen States and some of the later admitted ones,
and unearthing now and then a case in which the men
of that day had sketched out, though they saw but
dimly, a doctrine which has been of vast influence upon
our history. And then there followed for me the interest of seeking further light upon the particular instance
from other sources. Not so many cases in all were
brought to light by my study, but they were enough to
show that Marbury v. Madison was not, as so many
had thought it was, the *fons et origo* of our very remarkable judicial power.

My article once published, it became, of course, at
once public property, and its stones were ere long
taken down and used (so Huxley, I think, put it) as
the rubble for roads of study by others. It thus served
a good purpose, and some cases were added by students, or those I had found were further elucidated,
while for a time active interest rather ceased for me.
This, however, was again aroused when the partially
completed work of Brinton Coxe on "Judicial Power

and Unconstitutional Legislation" was put into my hands after his death, and at his request, for the purpose of my editing it. He had talked with me on the general subject, while I soon learned a deal from his pages; among other things that the American Doctrine was by no means the absolutely new departure in governmental science that my rather narrow path of study had led me to think it. Not many more years, then, went by before I learned that an onslaught was being made by some writers on our American beliefs and actions on this subject of more than a century. I answered (as did also others) these attacks in an article of 1906,[2] and in another of 1913;[3] but it is not for me to say with what success in point of reason.

Certainly, however, with none in point of effect, for our critics have gone on undeterred, in spite of all the very plain and palpable facts of our history. Their numbers have, moreover, beyond doubt increased. Those who consider and call themselves "Progressives" have, many of them, taken up the hue and cry, and to-day our ancient doctrine is traversed and certainly in danger of being rejected, or perhaps confessed and then avoided through some by-way. It is one more instance of that itch for mere change which is so conspicuously to be seen among our public men of to-day.

Some of the protagonists of the discovery that our American Doctrine was a Great Usurpation have, moreover, had the satisfaction in recent years of see-

[2] *American Law Review* (March-April, 1885), Vol. XL. pp. 641-670.
[3] *Ibid.*, Vol. XLVII, pp. 683-696.

ing their diatribes printed in one way or another at public expense, or even as part of the Congressional Record, then franked far and wide, to influence public opinion, while we conservatives of the Great Mob of our American one hundred millions only occasionally speak out, and then have no Public Printer back of us. It shows, again, how true is the belief that a clamorous minority will often drown by its vociferations the sober opinion of the real majority. And we who believe in this part of our inherited and long-tried system must not deceive ourselves. There is the gravest danger that this noisy minority will lead the country largely, even entirely, to abandon its canons and laws and to launch out upon evil ways, much to its detriment, precisely as a street mob will often follow courses far worse than the average desire of its members.

It is the conviction of this danger that has led me once more to take up the subject of Judicial Power. To-day many have treated the various phases of the origin of the American Doctrine, and a vast deal of matter bearing on its history and nature has been gathered together by various writers; but I feel that the subject will bear still another treatment. This should, in my opinion, be altogether historical in method, and some phases of the very early growth of that Doctrine are happily now far more accessible than was the case even less than a decade ago.

Early colonial doings prepared the ground, and the seed then planted was already sprouting at and before the Federal Convention, and then quickly grew into our American Doctrine almost as necessarily as the sowing of wheat results in the growth of the chief food of the world. It was an evolution, slowly made step by step, and long with little knowledge of whither it would lead, precisely as is the case with all such evolutions in public affairs, but we can see to-day (if we do not perversely shut our eyes) that the result was about as foreordained from the circumstances as is the possession of its wonderful power of scent to a pure-blooded pointer-puppy. In my opinion, the evidence accessible to-day is a demonstration, only less certain than those of astronomy and mathematics, that the Judiciary was plainly pointed out by our history for the vast function it has exercised, and that it was expected and intended, both by the Federal Convention and the opinion of the publicists of the day, to exercise that function.

Shall the American people abandon this principle at the very time when much of it is being adopted as desirable by many other growing peoples, and when the problems of government sure to follow on the vast war of to-day seem to promise more federations,— perhaps infinitely greater than any now known,— which will need some such system to hold the members quietly in control under ordinary circumstances? It is amazing how far and wide throughout the world our American Doctrine has spread; the reason for its dissemination being surely because it filled a need and offered a well-tried means, instead of being some supposed new panacea, which would almost certainly follow the course of most such cures, and break down in a few years.

Not only have Canada and Australia followed our lead in this matter, but the same has been the case in the still newer South African Republic, in New Zealand, and in Argentina, Bolivia, Colombia, Cuba, Mexico, Rumania and Venezuela, as well as in Finland as against a Russian law, while the very "Mother of Parliaments," after having watched the working of the system for several decades in one of her older offspring, has not only approved of it more recently for younger ones, but is now thinking of adopting it for the government of Great Britain herself, in the new relations with Ireland under the proposed Home Rule Bill.[4] France, too, we are told, is tending in the same direction. "In recent years," writes Prof. Garner of the University of Illinois, "there has been an interesting and very remarkable extension of judicial control over the administrative authorities in France," and this growth seems not to be at all confined to matters of administration alone but to extend to all branches of law, as well as to have the approval of many students of jurisprudence.[5] Verily, here is a

[4] I considered shortly the instances of Canada and Australia in 1906 in my article "Some Recent Attacks," etc., in 40 *American Law Review,* pp. 667, 668. See the same treated more fully in "Report of the Committee on the Duty of Courts to Refuse to Execute Statutes in Contravention of the Fundamental Law," presented at the 38th Annual Meeting of the New York State Bar Association, held at Buffalo, January 22 and 23, 1915, pp. 34-43. The other instances are taken from *ibid.,* pp. 43-50.

[5] James W. Garner's "Judicial Control of Administrative and Legislative Acts in France," in *American Political Science Review,* Vol. IX, pp. 637-665. Prof. Garner writes that the question

formidable array of practical endorsement to be somehow explained away by the critics of our American System.

And yet, in the face of all this, we are noisily urged by the "Progressives" to abandon our long-tried system, widely adopted though it has been by other peoples, and to drift off—into What? There are undoubtedly evils in our existing system, and the courts have made many an absurd and harmful decision; but the fire is hot as well as the frying-pan. Let Congress (and the State Legislatures?) have the right to pass what law it will, or what law its majority may please to think constitutional, and where shall we find ourselves? With all our roots entwined around the existence of the right of Judicial Review, how can Congress, untrammeled by that long-inherited principle, be trusted? Its members, and all the land, have too long depended on the courts to right the wrongs,—unwittingly, hastily, or in passion,—perpetrated upon the rights of a minority; and it is not in human nature that they should now cast off the customs grown up in a long course of years, and quickly become Constitutional students, or scrupulously careful of the rights of others.

Grave danger of radical and revolutionary courses lurk hidden in any such change; and we had best be very slow to make it, until we have carefully studied the matter in all its collateral consequences, or we may

has in recent years provoked widespread discussion, and "the American doctrine has been defended by many jurists," of whom he names twelve. "Prof. Duguit," he adds, "thinks it is only a question of time when the American practice will be introduced in France." See pp. 661 and 664.

well once more find ourselves in the predicament into which recent methods have so often led us; that of hastily adopting a half-thought-out new law and then soon awaking to the consciousness that the new condition is worse than the old one, and of longing to repeal the supposed sure-cure.

WILLIAM M. MEIGS.

PHILADELPHIA.

The Relation of the Judiciary to the Constitution

CHAPTER I

THE BRITISH COLONIES IN NORTH AMERICA

THE founding of the British Colonies in America was an event of vast importance to the world, and to the present study was of course absolutely vital. Those hardy immigrants to the wilds of the New World sprang from the loins of a people who had already laid the foundations of Popular Government. The colonists bore with them this great germinal principle, and their circumstances in the new home tended strongly to foster its growth. No paternal system at home guided and controlled their steps in America, nor was an organized system of society brought with them. There were of course leaders, who were looked up to and had far more power than the poor and lowly, but in the main their society was based on a democracy of a very advanced type for that day.

They had not only to conquer nature but also to establish a new government and a new social system.

Those that they had left could not be adopted, for the elements to which to attach them were quite wanting, and the colonists had to,—as they did,—reject some portions of the old, while at the same time they molded many other parts to their new surroundings. The different settlements varied in their solutions of these problems, but in every one popular government found a leading place. The individual bulked large. Add to this the often-aiding hand of the home government, which by no means let the colonies go off entirely on their own responsibility,—a hand that meant to guard them from themselves, as well as to exploit them and make them profitable to the home country,— and we have plenty of material with which to develop something very new.

It was rather a haphazard method, very wanting in unity of direction, as was indeed the system of the home-country as well. Both systems were governments of compromise. In neither was the Executive very strong, and that *preparedness,* of which we hear so much nowadays was conspicuous only by its absence.

In the early days in this country, the far more prepared French, guided by an Executive which was the State, owned in reality the Continent and ought to have forever remained its master; but despite the fact that they at first concentrated their energies far more quickly than the English, and long promised to control everything, the saving leaven of democracy gave the victory to the latter. That individualism, which is a part of democracy and which taught the Englishman and his colonist to take care of himself under all circumstances, was an interstitial force binding all the inhabitants together and bringing into play the utmost power of every single individual composing the society, much like the atomic force of matter, and it soon swept to ruin all the power of the French Executive and all its preparedness.

But of this only these few words in passing, in order to direct attention to some of the ingredients which were contained in the caldron in which was to originate along the Atlantic Coast of North America,—always from the old materials slowly shaped to our needs, with many a turbulent struggle, yet with no little conservatism,—much that was new in the administration of human affairs.

It has been said that the British did not mean to let their colonies drift off on their own course, but rather to use them for the profit of the home-country, in accordance with the ideas of the time. They well knew that raw colonists would pass many a callow law and adopt methods by no means wanted at home; and from the start the home government aimed to prevent this, in time developing a system for the purpose, which was, beyond doubt, of great influence in leading to that judicial power with which this book has to do.

Hence, in conferring, as English principles demanded should be done, the right to create something like a Parliament, the several colonies were by no means given a general power to legislate, but were in every case limited to the passing of laws consonant with their charter, or in accordance, as near as might be, with the laws of England; and means, which were in the main very effective, were found to enforce these limitations, especially as the colonies grew in population and power, and hence in the tendency to break away from restraints. The colonists were a stiff-necked people, and in numbers of cases managed to carry out their own wishes; but the people in the old home were also stiff-necked, and they held the colonial legislatures in many instances pretty closely to the limitations to which they had been subjected.

One of the methods of attaining this end was through the Privy Council, which ere long appointed a committee to examine the laws of the colonies and to report upon their legality. Not all the colonies were required, as Pennsylvania was, to submit their laws to the King in Council; but the Crown found ways by those indirect methods which often play a greater part in development than do positive provisions, to induce every one of our thirteen colonies to submit its laws to this scrutiny.

The Committee of the Privy Council, and later the Lords of Trade and Plantations and the Board of Trade, submitted the laws so sent to a most careful examination as to their legality,—or *constitutionality*, for this very word of modern times was already occasionally used. The laws were referred first to their counsel,—long regularly employed for this purpose,—and he scrutinized the alleged statute with that meticulous search for fault, which is so characteristic of the profession of the lawyer. If it was reported to violate the provisions of the charter in any way, or to concern a subject on which legislation was not authorized, or if it was contrary to some particular Act of Parliament, or was not in the main in accordance with the laws of England, the Committee of the Council or the Board of Trade would recommend its disallowance, and of course this recommendation would be followed by the King in Council. Full many a popular pet of legislation in various colonies came to an untimely end by this means; and the whole subject was one of much interest in the colonies, both to the mass of the people and to leading public men.

Quite a system grew up in the matter. The agents maintained in Great Britain by many of the colonies had for a main duty to see that the laws passed were not disallowed, and they always followed their course and appeared to argue the question of legality. At times some one having an interest against a law would call the attention of the Board of Trade, or of the King in Council, to an alleged want of legality in a particular statute; and then hearings would be had, arguments presented on both sides, and perhaps evidence taken, until the Board, with all these aids, should make its recommendation to the King. Those who complained against laws were very often merchants; and the reader can make a shrewd guess as to the character of many laws such as merchants would complain of. The easy and very prompt collection of debts was to their interest, while the colonists wanted to protect themselves from being ground too hard, and to allow debtors plenty of time. Various forms of bankruptcy laws, legal tender acts, stay-laws, statutes of limitation, provisions as to usury,—these were all favorites of the colonists; while the British merchant seemed often to want for himself the last pound of flesh of the unfortunate debtor.[1] It is a struggle doubtless as old as trading itself.

In late years several examinations have been made of English records relating to the practice and general methods employed in the scrutiny of colonial legislation by the King in Council. Of these, two very recent ones[2] are particularly extensive and careful, and have been relied upon for the purposes of this book. The results reached by both investigators are in general alike, and the thanks of American students are due to these two gentlemen for the long weeks of hard study they have devoted to their task in a foreign country and far from home.

The colonial essays at legislation were indeed subject to the closest examination,—and they needed it. Often crude beyond belief,—with one department of government making the widest incursions into the field of another, and with at times far too little regard paid to vested rights and even to fundamental principles of liberty,—those early legislative assemblies did certainly need a guiding hand, even though it be the case that they were at times far too much cabin'd, cribb'd, confin'd, by their guardian and stepmother in her own interest. They were as yet by no means fit for

[1] Oliver Morton Dickerson's "American Colonial Government," pp. 252, 253.
[2] Oliver Morton Dickerson, "American Colonial Government," "The Review of American Colonial Legislation by the King in Council," by Elmer Beecher Russell (Columbia University Studies in History, Economics and Public Law, Vol. LXIV, Number 2).

what has been well called "the responsible business of legislation."

The Board of Trade had regular counsel, to whom the laws were referred, and we are told by one of these recent students that the question most frequently asked by the Board of their counsel was as to

the legality, or what might now be termed the constitutionality of legislation. Had the colonial legislature exceeded its power and authority in passing the law? Were its provisions unwarranted under the terms of the provincial charter, or in conflict with an Act of Parliament? The Board inquired, for example, whether two acts of North Carolina were proper consistently with the just rights of the inhabitants and the constitution of said Province? And three private acts granting decrees of divorce, they referred to the attorney and solicitor upon a matter of doubt whether the legislature of the Province of Massachusetts Bay or any other Colony has a power of passing Laws of this nature, and consequently whether these laws are not of themselves null and void. And, to give one example among many, a naturalization law of New Jersey was sent to the solicitor with an inquiry, as to how far it was consistent with the act of Parliament of "12 Charles II . . . or other acts of Parliament."[3]

Again, we are told that

In numerous instances, the Council declared laws inconsistent with the terms of a provincial charter, and therefore void. Several objectionable Acts passed by the proprietary governments of the Carolinas were annulled upon the broad ground that being repugnant to

[3] Russell's "Review of Colonial Legislation," pp. 63, 64.

the laws of England, they constituted a violation of the law-making power conferred by the charter. . . . Massachusetts lost several laws which were deemed inconsistent with her charter. In these cases, however, disallowance was based upon more specific grounds. . . . Jackson, who, as king's counsel, loved to play with large abstractions, frequently based his criticism upon the broad ground that the law constituted a violation of the British constitution, or, in other words, that it failed to maintain the English standard of legal justice.[4]

A law of North Carolina, enacting that no one but barristers of five years in one of the Inns of Court in England should become a judge, was disallowed, because "this was deemed 'an unconstitutional restraint upon the power of appointing judges.' "[5] And a law in the Bahamas prohibiting any appeal to the Privy Council "was deemed 'altogether inconsistent with the constitution of the Colony.' "[6]

The general result is said to have been that

in such policies as the crown chose to maintain consistently and without compromise the colonies learned to acquiesce; for against a disallowance followed by an instruction to the Governor forbidding his assent to any future act of like purport, the popular party, as a rule, could make little or no headway. . . . By reason of many annulments the colonists learned to respect the personal rights and private property of individuals and to

[4] Russell's "Review of Colonial Legislation," pp. 147, 150.
[5] *Ibid.*, p. 189.
[6] *Ibid.*, p. 191.

abide by the forms and larger precedents of English law.[7]

A large number of colonial laws came to an untimely end by virtue of this sifting process. Of about 8,500 acts submitted by the continental colonies, some 469 (or 5.5 per cent) were disallowed. The percentage varied widely in different colonies, but was in general so large as to bring the whole subject to popular attention, as will shortly be shown from the records of the day.[8]

There was another means by which the home-country held the far-distant colonies to methods in general consonance with her own, and of which she approved. The system of appeals from colonial judicial decisions to the same Privy Council, which (as has just been shown) disallowed statutes, is referred to. These appeals were, of course, not of daily occurrence, but they were in quite sufficient number to make a deep impression. Between 1680 and 1780, "the most significant period of the operation of the appellate system," we are told that no less than 265 cases reached the Privy Council from the continental colonies of England. Seventy-eight of these cases came from Rhode Island, 53 from Virginia, 44 from Massachusetts, 21 from New York, 13 from Pennsylvania, 12 each from New Jersey and New Hampshire, and 9 from Connecticut. There were 76 reversals.[9]

[7] *Ibid.*, pp. 204, 205.
[8] *Ibid.*, p. 221, or Dickerson's "Colonial Government," p. 227. See *infra.* pp. 26-29.
[9] "Colonial Appeals to the Privy Council," by Arthur Meier Schlesinger, *Political Science Quarterly*, Vol. XXVIII, p. 446.

This judicial method of control was, of course, to the scientific lawyer quite different from the executive disallowance of laws already referred to, but to the layman, uneducated in the mysteries of law and politics, the difference was far from plain. To the popular mind, the two methods must have seemed much the same, and each resulted in the undoing of some policy in public affairs that the colony concerned had enacted. Even in modern days learned historians differ upon the question whether some particular instance enacted not far from two hundred years ago falls into the one class or the other.[10]

The whole system which we have been considering, and particularly the veto which the Privy Council often put on laws passed and most strongly desired in the colonies, was very vital to the dwellers in the New World. Bitter contests arose in some cases over it, and in numerous instances the hard-headed colonists struggled in many ways, after the disallowance, to secure their own will and get into legal form on the statute-books laws and principles which the mass of their people eagerly desired. Laws, which had been once disallowed, were often reënacted, perhaps with some little modification so as to look less like defiance, and this would even be done several times in succession; thereby in some instances the law would be maintained

Cf. "Appeals from Colonial Courts to the King in Council, with Especial Reference to Rhode Island," by Harold D. Haseltine, in "Annual Report of the American Hist. Assn.," 1894, p. 337.
[10] Coxe's "Judicial Power and Unconstitutional Legislation," p. 212, holds the action to have been partly legislative and partly judicial.

in effect during the long period that often elapsed
between its colonial enactment and the arrival of news
that it had been again disallowed.[11]

There were other devices or accidents by which the
colonies had occasionally a measure of success. Sometimes, notice of disallowance failed to reach the colonial authorities, or possibly the latter intentionally
neglected to enter the disallowance upon the law books.
Thus Gov. Cadwallader Colden wrote to the Board in
1761 that he was

> told that several acts in Basket's edition of the acts of
> New York in 1718 are noted to be repealed, of which
> not the least evidence appears anywhere in the Province.
> . . . I make no doubt the judges continue to proceed
> upon them as of force.

A Virginia law, which had been disallowed, was in
reality carried out for nearly thirty years. One in
New Hampshire had a still longer unauthorized existence of over half a century; and the repeal of a
Massachusetts law "establishing the township of Dan-
vers" was for one reason or another never observed
in the colony.[12]

Many of these difficulties and strange results were
doubtless owing to the slowness of communication in
that day. It is not easy for us to realize how utterly
unreliable this was, but there was, for instance, no
regular mail service of any kind to or from the colonies

[11] Russell's "Review of Colonial Legislation," pp. 210-212.
[12] Ibid., pp. 212, 213. "New York Colonial Documents," Vol.
VII, pp. 454, 455.

until 1755. Letters from North Carolina, we are told, went usually by way of Virginia, and letters for Virginia frequently came out by way of New York. Even the colonies having direct communication with England were not much better off, for vessels came in quite unannounced and went off whenever ready. In 1754 the Board wrote the Governor of North Carolina that it had not heard from him for three years; and he answered a year later that he was surprised at their communication, which had just reached him, and added that he had been a regular correspondent. His letters may have been lost, or perhaps he was lying; but other communications of his seem to show that two years and a half were required at times for a letter to cross the ocean, and that letters to him often passed from hand to hand all the way across Virginia and North Carolina. Those for England had often to be entrusted to the captain of any sailing vessel, bound for another port, and he would there have to transfer them to some captain, by whom they might finally reach England. And even in the home-country there were great delays, and letters occasionally lay for long periods at the Custom House.[13] We need not wonder that the consequent delays were such as to lead to the most incongruous results.

The instances, which have been cited, of laws disallowed and of reversals of judicial decrees of the colonies, though they are far from numerous, indicate plainly enough that the main principles on which

[13] Dickerson's "American Colonial Government," pp. 133-137.

they rested were of vital interest to the colonists, and by no means known only to public men. Other indications, too, tell the same story, and show that the disallowance, and the setting aside of laws by the distant power across the seas, entered into the daily life of the colonists, and was widely known and understood among the masses of the people. Thus, letters from some Governors are extant, telling the Board of Trade that the disallowance of a popular law had excited considerable ill-feeling against the merchant-class, which had been active in breaking down the law in question; and, again, governors' letters, and even protests from the assemblies, show restiveness and resentment arising from the loss of some colonial law eagerly desired by popular opinion. In at least one instance, a riot resulted from the disallowance.[14]

The fear that laws might meet with this mishap was, moreover, constantly before colonial legislators; and I think it is well known that the advocates of special statutes were often warned in debate that the proposed measure was beyond the powers conferred by their charter, and would, if enacted, be held void for this reason. At least, the legislatures had the fear of such a result ever before their eyes, and took means to avoid it. In Pennsylvania, for instance, where a period of five years was allowed for the submission of laws to the King, the legislators would pass a law limited as to its duration to a shorter period, and would then, about the time of its expiration, re-

[14] Russell's "Review of Colonial Legislation," pp. 77, 221.

enact it. Sometimes they were even bolder and would openly reënact a disallowed law, in at least much the same words.[15]

One more proof of the wide knowledge of all this among the people comes from a much later source. The Declaration of Independence was a wonderful paper and full of stirring thoughts, but it was also meant as an appeal to the feelings and prejudices of the masses. The lawyers, who drew and adopted it, omitted few elements which would tend to add to its popularity, and in the fact that no less than eight of its counts against the Crown were based on the disallowance of statutes, claimed to be essentially needed by the colonies, may doubtless be found one more conclusive proof that the disallowance of statutes by the Crown in Council, was in its day a matter of vital moment to the colonists and well-known to the vast majority of those who had any knowledge whatsoever of public affairs.

The colonists came insensibly and quite inevitably to feel in their daily life, that apparent laws passed in strict accordance with all the forms by their legislature, and often after long popular agitation, might turn out to be no laws at all but void, because not authorized to be passed under the terms of a fundamental law of higher authority. To them, all their legislatures were closely restricted and could not legally (or, as we now say, "constitutionally") violate the

[15] "Chronicles of Pennsylvania, 1688-1748," by Charles P. Keith, Vol. I, pp. 154, 155.

limitations of the instrument under which they existed. If the effort to do so were made, another agency would solemnly annul the statute passed and declare it void.

CHAPTER II

THE grooves or ruts of thought of various ages of the world differ widely, and it is a very great error to cast back modern beliefs and try to read by their light the civilization and methods of a past time. The frame of thought, the very language in which we talk of government or any other agency, has a vital influence upon our beliefs. The theory of man in a state of nature, which had such vogue after Rousseau's time, was doubtless from one point of view nonsense,—for no such state ever did or could exist,—but it had none the less a potent influence on the beliefs of humanity, and aided greatly to spread afar a belief in the Rights of Man. That Democracy for which the world is now struggling and the great humanitarian spirit of recent times owe it a deep debt.

The Age of the American Colonies was far from looking upon governmental matters and theories as we do to-day. The idea of three departments of government, so clearly separated as we now think them, was not yet accepted as an axiom. The fundamental basis, moreover, on which legislation must rest, was looked upon from a very different standpoint from that which we now occupy. Probably, the Puritan, the Quaker, and the more fundamentally aristocratic Southern colonists, would all have been equally unable to comprehend a view which denies the necessity and reality of the distinction between *mala in se* and *mala prohibita.* The theocratic or theological influence of the times was enormous.

In some of the New England colonies, the controlling elements were for a time exclusively theologians, who even announced that human laws were unnecessary, as the Bible furnished a complete guide to human action. Other elements of like beliefs were floating around, too, in that day. The doctrine of fundamental principles implanted by God, which had been held in the Middle Ages, had not yet died out, and perhaps it was not for that matter so very different from the famous dictum of Coke, about to be mentioned, or, again, from the views enforced by our own courts to-day, when declining to carry out a law which they look upon as in violation of great, but rather intangible, primordial principles of liberty. These latter are now to some extent crystallized in the general phrases of the Fourteenth Amendment.

One very important idea of that time must be further examined. Coke's dictum in Bonham's case,—that the common law doth control Acts of Parliament and declare them void, when against common right and reason,—is referred to. This ruling of the mighty common lawyer received some scattering confirmation in a few early English cases, and has even found an endorsement to-day,[1] but seems to be entirely unmaintainable. The cases which give the doctrine apparent support are in reality but ones in which the court did what any court will and ought to do: seek to interpret a statute in such a way that no absurd or grossly unjust result shall flow therefrom. One instance, put many years ago, is that of an Act ordaining that the same person shall be party and judge which (so the court said)[2] would be a void Act; but not only do cases arise in which a judge with an interest in the decision must sit or no decision can ever be had, but the better opinion clearly is that in that day, as now, if Parliament should plainly and positively so enact, no court would dream of undertaking to stand in its way, and, of course, any court would be utterly powerless, if the legislative body should insist.

Such decisions as that in Bonham's case appear to be but the vagaries of an able man, swept away by the pomp of his office and by an overweening worship for that which a later judge, strangely enough, called "the perfection of human reason." It flies, too, in the face of actual experience; for what could be more absolutely against common reason, and in violation of all the rules of liberty and justice, than those acts of attainder which occur here and there in English

[1] "Report of the Committee on the Duty of Courts to Refuse to Execute Statutes in Contravention of the Fundamental Law," presented at the 38th Annual Meeting of the New York State Bar Association, held at the City of Buffalo on the 22nd and 23rd of January, 1913, p. 15 *et seq.*

[2] City of London *v.* Wood, 12 Modern, 687.

history and in that of our colonial period? To enact
that John Doe shall be judge in a case in which he is
a party, is certainly very unjust, nor can the violation
be justified, unless absolute necessity compels it. The
injustice of such legislation, however, pales before that
of an Act which rudely seizes a citizen and, without
even a pretense of hearing or trial, condemns him,—
often on common rumor,—to be drawn and quartered,
to have all his possessions forfeited, and to suffer that
corruption of blood which falls mainly on his inno-
cent offspring. While these instances of attainders
stare us in the face, the doctrine of Bonham's case
must surely be classed as a vagary, or else it must
be regarded simply as a judicial instance of juggling
words, so as to avoid a very unjust result, which the
judge is convinced was not in reality intended by the
legislative authority.

But again here, as has not infrequently been seen
in human history, this particular doctrine, though quite
false in essence, has had no little influence. Our
colonial lawyers seem to have believed in it, and it
fitted in well with the Middle Ages' idea of fundamental principles implanted by God, and, again, in
the fertile soil of "Man in a State of Nature."
Probably, also, the ultra-theological view of public
affairs tended to its acceptance. At a very early date
in our history it was widely admitted in at least part
of the country.

In the controversy of Massachusetts with the other
Confederate Colonies of New England in 1653 upon the

right of the Confederation to make offensive war, all parties agreed that any acts or orders manifestly unjust or against the law of *God* were not binding. . . . In 1688 "the men of Massachusetts did much quote Lord Coke.[3]"

We shall find, too, resort to it made by our public men in some few instances preceding the Revolution, where some law very obnoxious to the principles of liberty was under argument in the colonial courts, and, again, against the Stamp Act.

The history of our colonial period has not yet been sufficiently studied for one to know positively whether in those days the courts in this country rendered occasional decisions approaching our modern ones on the branch of constitutional law with which this book is concerned. A vast deal of turning over of dusty records must yet be done before this point can be settled. Some writers think the evidence is that there were such, and cite certain colonial cases as in point, and vague gropings in the general direction are certainly to be found in these, while some rather closer approaches have been apparently brought to light by the recent investigators of the records of the English Board of Trade; but neither of these classes furnishes, in my opinion, any substantial support to the American Doctrine. It is noteworthy, too, in this

[3] Article on "Writs of Assistance," printed in Quincy's Reports (said in the Preface of 1864 to be by Horace Gray, Jr., of the Boston bar, later a Justice of the Supreme Court of the United States), Appendix I, p. 527, footnote. Lambert MS. quoted in Bancroft's "History," Vol. II, p. 428, is cited as authority for the matter in sub-quotations at the end of my quotation.

connection that, when the system in question was being forged into shape (at and about 1787), no hint reaches us of a knowledge among the public men of the day as to decisions of this character having been rendered by colonial courts.

It is not altogether easy to understand how they could have been avoided at times under, for instance, the British statute providing specifically that colonial laws or customs repugnant to any Act of Parliament having relation to the colonies, should be null and void,[4] and it may yet possibly turn out that instances of the kind or very close to it, did occur in this connection. It will shortly be shown that the nearest known approach seems to be in a case of this character, where the colonial courts had before them two conflicting laws in relation to the same subject, and thus were apparently almost forced to decide whether to carry out the law of the colonial legislature or the specific and differing provision of an Act of Parliament in regard to the value of coins.

Probably one reason for the absence of such decisions in general is to be found in the fact that by the date when the colonies came to have any real importance, our stiff-necked colonial ancestors had, in the main, succeeded in securing the control of their own affairs. It is true that in some colonies the judges were actually named by the Crown, but this was by no means always the case; and even in such

[4] "The American Doctrine of Judicial Supremacy," by Charles Grove Haines, p. 65, citing "Statutes of the Realm," Vol. VII, p. 105 (1696).

instances the nominees were likely to be citizens of the colony itself.

There was one other vital matter in the connection: The lower houses in the legislatures held the purse-strings for the judges, as well as for other officers, and this has always been a potent influence with the sons of men. This result was the culmination of a long struggle in which the Governors and the Crown appointing them had sought to drive the legislatures to provide permanent salaries, but with no measure of success. The lower houses stood out against any such plan, with a most dogged persistence; and long succeeded, too, in making the commissions of the judges read "during good behavior," instead of "during pleasure," as the Crown wanted. They were, it is true, in the end defeated as to this latter point, but they had their own Treasurer, by whose hands salaries were paid; and these salaries were subject to frequent regulation by the legislature.

And the "legislature" meant the popular branch. By 1765, so we are told, the Councils had been robbed of their chief legislative powers, and

Judges and other officers had become dependent upon the lower house. . . . There is but little doubt that the power of the Assembly to fix salaries rendered all the judges practically dependent upon that body, except in the few instances in which they received their salaries from the crown. In New York the salaries were varied from time to time, and in one case apparently for the purpose of showing disapproval of a decision of the Supreme Court.[5]

The judges thus came to be dependent in a vital matter on the colonial authorities, and would probably have been slow to decide that laws passed by their actual master were void because of being in violation of some law, or charter, which owed its force to a power on the other side of tempestuous seas, three thousand miles away,—a distance in modern times of five days or little more, but then of long, long months, or even of years. But this is thrown out merely as a suggestion or guess as to the reason for the entire absence of a line of decisions of which we should expect at least to find instances, and which the student of days to come may yet learn did exist.

Let us now examine the few cases, or hints that have come down to us across the centuries; and, in the first place, it will be best to consider such as are preserved in our own records.

One very early case in a colonial court does grope around the general subject, and uses language not

[5] Dickerson's "Colonial Government," pp. 11 and 195, and see generally 160-207. "Introduction" to Geo. Chalmers's "History of the Revolt of the American Colonies," Vol. II, pp. 52-56, is to the same effect. He writes that between about 1720 and 1730 the New York Assembly seized all powers, made every officer dependent on them, and cut the Chief Justice's salary from 300 to 250 pounds a year, "pretending that they did not object to his administration, but that the colony, now less wealthy than formerly, was unable to maintain so great an establishment." They also, Chalmers adds, weakened the supreme court of common law, and then proceeded to overturn the chancery courts, resolving that they had "been established by incompetent powers."

entirely dissimilar from that to be found in judicial rulings of to-day; but it is, in my opinion, far from being in point, or a *decision* of the question in the judicial sense. Giddings *v.* Brown is referred to,—a case that was decided by Magistrate Symonds in Massachusetts in 1657. It is far from clear, like many another case; however, one point plain enough is that the enactment attacked was not at all a statute passed by the Legislature but a mere ordinance of the town authorities of Ipswich. They had levied a sum on the inhabitants to buy or build a house for a new parson. This was resisted by Giddings, and Symonds held that he could not be forced to pay.

The idea which Symonds seems to have acted on was that Giddings' property was simply being taken from him and handed over to another. This, he said, could not be done even by Parliament, though it may tax the whole country, but "it is against a fundamental law in nature to be compelled to pay that which others do give." Even in England, he adds, citing Finch, a law which is "repugnant to fundamentall law" is void; and he cites similar colonial decisions made by a town (not by a court) in regard to such questions, for instance, as a levy to bring in a surgeon to reside in the town. Symonds's decision was later reversed in the General Court, and the levy held valid.[6]

[6] Giddings *v.* Brown, cited in "The English Common Law in the American Colonies," by Paul Samuel Reinsch, in "Select Essays in Anglo-American History," Vol. I, pp. 376, 377. Mr. Reinsch refers for a full report of the case to the "Hutchinson Papers," Vol. II, p. 1 *et seq.,* whence my account is of course taken.

A footnote to the case suggests that the real question at issue was whether an act of the supreme authority empowering the majority of the inhabitants of a town to tax a non-consenting minority was or was not contrary to the fundamental laws of government. If the legislative authority had formally authorized the towns to do this, the case would technically be far more nearly in point; for then the town ordinance would be indirectly the act of the supreme power itself. However, the long and rambling report fails to show this fact, and the judge certainly acted upon no such theory, but upon the conviction that the ordinance was contrary to natural justice. In other words, he applied that later favorite of the colonists: Coke's doctrine that statutes against common right and reason are void. There was at the time a controversy in the colony whether spiritual guides should be entirely dependent on voluntary contributions, or whether an objecting minority should be forced equally to pay. In the following century, a Massachusetts law of 1722, levying a tax on Quaker towns for the support of Congregational ministers, was of course not set aside in Massachusetts, but it was disallowed by the King in Council.[7]

[7] Dickerson's "Colonial Government," pp. 267-269. See, however (*infra,* pp. 42, 43), the opinion of Yorke and Talbot in 1732 in relation to a like tax complained of by some members of the English church, who had been sent out to America. "Historical Collections of the American Colonial Church," by Wm. Stevens Perry, Vol. III, Massachusetts, pp. 274-288, or "Statutes at Large of Pennsylvania," Vol. V, pp. 735-737. I am indebted for this reference and for other aid in this general matter, to Prof. Elmer Beecher Russell.

The well-known case of Frost v. Leighton [8] has also been thought to be in point, but does not seem to be so in reality. It is true that in this instance the Superior Court of Judicature of Massachusetts Bay declined to enforce an order issued by the King in Council, alleging as its reason that "the powers of the court derived through the charter and the laws passed to carry the same into effect, were in the judgment of the court inadequate for that purpose." But in reality, in so far as this action is not to be classed as bold defiance, the language was merely a subterfuge, and at other stages of the litigation, the Massachusetts court simply declined to carry out English decrees in the case on what have been deservedly called "disingenuous" grounds. At one time they complimented counsel on his suggestion of certain very technical reasons, which had "relieved them from their embarrassment.[9]"

The truth is that the case was but one in a long struggle by the colonial authorities to prevent appeals to the Privy Council, or to rob them of all effect. In the particular instance, the authorities in the new country wriggled and twisted in every way, first in order to prevent any appeal to the Privy Council, and, when that effort failed, to prevent the decree,—or rather the decrees, for there were several of them,— from having the least effect.

They were indeed a bold and self-assertive people, already far along on the high road to independence,

[8] "The Case of Frost v. Leighton," by Andrew McF. Davis in American Hist. Review, Vol. II (Jany., 1897), pp. 229-240.
[9] Ibid., pp. 234, 238.

and we are told that about the last step in this lengthy controversy was that, when the Governor sent two orders of the Privy Council to the court, complaining that nothing had yet been done in the matter, though the legal form of issuing a summons to show cause was gone through with,—"it is doubtful whether even this perfunctory recognition of the governor's complaint was actually performed." The litigation had then been pending, and all the efforts of the home authorities successfully resisted for seven years,[10] nor need we wonder that the Secretary of the Board of Trade was informed at much the same time, from another colony, that this latter possession was aiming at "nothing less than being independent of the kingdom of Great Britain, as fast as they can.[11]

One other possible indication must be mentioned here, though it is far too vague to rely upon in a matter of history. In New York in 1691, after the end of Leisler's rebellion, the Assembly alone undertook to enact that many theretofore undoubted laws of the province were "null void and of none effect," and this extraordinary resolution was not even presented to the Governor and Council for their concurrence.[12] Such were now and then the incomprehensible methods of our ancestors in colonial days, and surely this instance bears out what has been said in

[10] Schlesinger's "Appeals to the Privy Council," "Political Science Quarterly," Vol. XXVIII, pp. 434-437.
[11] "Introduction" to "History of the Revolt of the American Colonies," by Geo. Chalmers, Vol. II, pp. 55-56.
[12] John R. Brodhead's "History of New York," Vol. II, pp. 643, 644.

these pages, that they needed a guiding and helping hand. It was to this resolution that Gov. Cadwallader Colden had reference, when he wrote in 1759:

By the first Act or Resolve of the first Assembly after the Revolution, a power is assumed of repealing Laws without the concurrence of the other branches of the Legislature, *or a Judicial power of declaring them void.* A Power which in no wise belonged to them: and which, if countenanced, may be highly prejudicial both to the Crown and the Subject; and yet this usurped power has, in this instance, taken effect ever since.[13]

I have placed in italics the words in Colden's letter, which seem so indicative, and it is certainly not easy to understand how he came, in referring to laws of the Legislature, to speak of "a Judicial power of declaring them void," unless the colonial courts had in that instance exercised the power referred to, or, at least, unless some such power in the Judiciary was talked of among the men of the time.

It remains to consider the instances which have been so recently discovered in the records of the Board of Trade in England. But it should be said, in the first place, that it is clear that the English lawyers,—and hence, presumably, the American lawyers also,—well knew the system by which colonial laws were occasionally held unauthorized and void by the English courts, as well as by the King in Council. Thus, Yorke and Talbot, in an opinion of 1732, upon the complaint of members of the English Church, as to

[13] "New York Historical Society Collections," 1869, pp. 203-211.

whether Massachusetts laws authorizing a levy on all inhabitants for the support of the Congregational Church were void, wrote that the laws could not then be *disallowed* by the Crown, adding, however:

If they were really void in themselves on this account, yet no Extrajudicial Declaration that they are so would be conclusive, but the only Method of bringing that matter to a Determination would be by some Judicial Proceeding.[14]

Similarly, Pratt and Yorke wrote in an opinion of 1750 that, though in general an act must be approved or disallowed by the Crown as a whole, yet particular provisions in violation of an Act of Parliament may be void *ab initio,* and added:

These are cases the decision of which does not depend on the exercise of a discretionary prerogative, but may arise judicially and must be determined by general rules and the constitution of England. And upon this ground it is that in some instances whole acts of assembly have been declared void in the courts of Westminster Hall, and by his Majesty in council upon appeals from the plantations.[15]

One record has been brought to light, showing that at least one judge in this country had some idea of the matter in 1742, and was in doubt what a court ought to do, when a colonial statute repugnant to

[14] "Historical Collections of the American Colonial Church," by Wm. Stevens Perry, Vol. III, Massachusetts, pp. 274-288.
[15] "Statutes at Large of Pennsylvania," Vol. V, pp. 735-737.

the laws of England was an essential element in some case before it.   Chief Justice Whitaker, of South Carolina, sent a representation to the Board of Trade in that year, in which he wrote at some length of the courts of law, and then went on substantially as follows:

> Sometimes acts have been made in the Parliament not only contrary to the King's instruction and prerogative, but repugnant to the laws of England.   Are these laws void from the beginning or only voidable by his Majesty's disallowance?   *What are judges to do when they are pleaded in evidence?* [16] Is repugnance to the laws of England to be understood of the Common or Statute law or of the Common Law as altered, explained or enlarged by Statutes, and what obligation has the statute law of England in the Plantations? . . . Can Acts of Assembly which have been confirmed by the Crown be repealed or altered by subsequent acts before such subsequent acts have been confirmed by the Crown? [17]

One other indication of the feeling on this general subject in South Carolina has been preserved, and is

[16] Italics mine.

[17] For this instance, which seems to me to show pretty plainly that such questions must have presented themselves at times to inquiring minds, I am entirely indebted to Prof. Elmer Beecher Russell. Upon my inquiring whether his notes made in England contained anything further upon the general subject of the action of colonial courts than is mentioned in his "Review of American Colonial Legislation," and especially at the end of footnote 3 in *ibid.*, p. 137, he kindly sent me this and a number of other memoranda he had made. My quotations are from his letter to me, which contains his notes as made abroad from the English records, but these (he writes me) are not *verbatim* copies but his summation. The reference to the Board of Trade records for this instance is C o/5—369-118 and 370—H34. 26 Jan., 1742.

strikingly similar to that just cited. In 1768 the author of an article on representation and the power of their assembly in the matter, writing at a time when the assembly had undertaken to reduce the representation in some parishes, argued that the right of representation rested on the English constitution, could only be granted by the King, and could never be revoked. Continuing, he said:

Being a part of the constitution, the Assembly had no power over it. In the writer's own words, "the constitution is as much above the reach of an act of assembly as Mt. Ossa is to a molehill." [18]

In addition to these hints, from Chief Justice Whitaker and the unknown writer in South Carolina just cited, one actual instance has been found in the Board of Trade records, in which it seems fairly clear that in a case of the nature put by Whitaker of South Carolina, the courts of Massachusetts and of New Hampshire about 1711 carried out an Act of Parliament in preference to a differing prior law of their own province in the same matter, which had been perfectly valid before the Act of Parliament, and had not been formally repealed.

This instance arose in the following way: The colonies had long been in the habit of passing laws to regulate the value of foreign coins, with the aim of

[18] Wm. A. Schaper's "Representation and Sectionalism in South Carolina," in "Annual Report of American Historical Association," 1900, Vol. I, pp. 230 *et seq. See* especially p. 347. There had been repeated efforts by the Assembly to alter the representation, and several such laws had been disallowed.

securing a circulating medium, but the Crown had always disallowed these, and finally issued a proclamation specifically regulating the coin values in the colonies, and not long thereafter an Act of Parliament to the same effect was passed. This was the end of the matter, as there was already a general Act [19] upon the statute-book, providing specifically that colonial laws, or customs, repugnant to any Act of Parliament having relation to the colonies should be null and void. In 1697, Massachusetts had passed an act to regulate the values of foreign coins, and this had been confirmed by the Crown in council. Then came the King's proclamation of 1702; but the Attorney-General of England gave it as his opinion that the confirmed colonial law was still of effect, despite the royal proclamation. Still another question arose, however, after the passage of the Act of Parliament of 1704 regulating the values, because of the general statute providing for the nullity of provincial laws differing from one enacted by Parliament.

How was this nullity to be ascertained and declared? If the colonial courts were to settle the question by examining and weighing the two opposing legislative acts,—of their Legislature and of Parliament,—to find out which was the fundamental and superior, and then to enter a decree based on the conclusion that one or the other was unauthorized and void, their decisions would come very close to the American Doctrine, and we are told in this instance, on the evidence

[19] Haines's "American Doctrine," p. 65, citing "Statutes of the Realm," Vol. VII, p. 105 (1696).

of a letter to the Board of Trade from the Governor of Massachusetts, preserved in the British records, that

After the passing of the Act of Parliament, the provincial courts, at least, appear to have followed the values prescribed therein.[20]

It is impossible to-day to go further into this question, and it must be left to the future to follow out the indication, in order to learn whether or not the courts of our colonies did undertake, in more than a very few,—or perhaps even a single instance,—to examine the relative value of conflicting laws upon the same subject passed by two legislative bodies, and to decide in a proper case that the law passed by their own Legislature was void, because unauthorized by a more fundamental charter, or Act of Parliament.

[20] Russell's "Review," etc., p. 137, footnote 3, citing C o/5—323, F, 14. C o/5—913, p. 285; 29 January, 1711. In this case again Prof. Russell has very kindly given me a more extensive detail of what his notes made in England contain. Lieut.-Gov. Usher of New Hampshire had written the Board of Trade that the Act of Parliament relating to foreign coins was being violated, and then Governor Dudley of Massachusetts wrote them on November 15, 1710, going into the history of the laws. The colonial law was of 1697 and prescribed "the former usage" of 17 pennyweight, while the King's Proclamation of 1702 fixed 17½ pennyweight, and the Act of Parliament of 1704 confirmed this. Dudley wrote that "Since then all courts have given judgment at 17½ and the Treasury can receive no more. Usher ought to know this. It is true also of New Hampshire." The Board in a reply to Dudley of Jany. 29, 1711 (Russell's "Review," citing *ibid.,* p. 322), "express themselves as satisfied with what he writes in regard to coin." The quotation in my text is from Russell's "Review" at the page indicated, and those in this footnote are from his letter to me, which contains (as already said) not *verbatim* transcripts from the records but his summation of what they contain.

CHAPTER III

FUNDAMENTAL LAW AND COKE'S DOCTRINE DURING REVOLUTIONARY DAYS. CONFLICTING LEGISLA- TION OF THE PERIOD AND ITS EFFECT ON PUBLIC OPINION

PROBABLY a people seldom or never altogether abandons the fundamental principles of its creed in regard to governmental affairs. They may, doubt- less, in the course of centuries take up many new be- liefs, and in a time of stress and revolution may even suddenly alter their principles so enormously that these will be hard to recognize, but the old is pretty sure to survive in some form and to be used as a constituent element in the new edifice.

Such was, I think, emphatically the case with our ancestors. The race continued to breed true to its stock and to its environment. They hardly could have shed My Lord Coke's doctrine of void laws and the older doctrine of fundamental principles implanted by God; for here was a theory of public affairs right at hand, which had infiltrated itself into their minds, and which offered an easy method of escape from unauthorized statutes. We shall see how quickly they had resort to it, under the swelling of that spirit of independence which reached its culmination in 1776, though it had long before been planted in their nature and had already had a sturdy growth.[1]   Those active, thinking, determined men wanted a justification for their actions; they felt forced to hold their people united; and the best defense at hand was one that was a sort of birthright of belief.

When, then, early in the second half of the eighteenth century, an effort was made in the higher courts of Massachusetts to issue general search-warrants, or "Writs of Assistance," to aid the Crown authorities in ferreting out smuggling, by means of house to house terrorizing, the old inherited belief was by no means forgotten, and James Otis based his argument against the writs on the claim that they violated English liberty and "the fundamental principles of law."   Mere notes of his speech, written down by John Adams, survive, but these abstract him in part as follows:

As to acts of Parliament.   An Act against the constitution is void; an act against natural equity is void; and if an act of Parliament should be made, in the very words of this petition, it would be void.   The executive courts must pass such acts into disuse [referring to Viner]. . . . Reason of the common law to control an act of Parliment.[2]

[1] Hosts of facts in proof of this could easily be gathered, but the instance (cited *ante,* p. 41) of the Attorney-General writing from New York in 1728 that the colony was aiming at "nothing less than being independent of the kingdom of Great Britain, as fast as they can," is enough here.

[2] John Adams's "Works," Vol. II, pp. 124-125, and Appendix, pp. 521-525.   See also Quincy's (Mass.) Reports, Appendix I, pp. 395-540, for article by the late Justice Gray.

And in a pamphlet [3] of a few years later (1764), Otis wrote:

If the reasons that can be given against an act are such as plainly demonstrate that it is against *natural* equity, the executive courts will adjudge such act void. It may be questioned by some, though I make no doubt of it, whether they are not obliged by their oaths to adjudge such act void. . . . To say the parliament is absolute and arbitrary, is a contradiction. . . . The supreme power in a state is *jus dicere* only; *jus dare,* strictly speaking, belongs alone to GOD. Should an act of parliament be against any of *his* natural laws, which are *immutably* true, *their* declaration would be contrary to eternal truth, equity and justice and consequently void: and so it would be adjudged by the parliament itself, when convinced of their mistake. Upon this great principle, parliaments repeal such acts, as soon as they find they have been mistaken. . . . When such mistake is evident and palpable . . . the judges of the executive courts have declared the act "of a whole parliament void."

Far off to the South, too, about a decade later (1772), the same argument was advanced by George Mason, as against a law of Virginia of 1682 for the sale of the descendants of Indian women as slaves. The statute, he contended,

was originally void in itself, because it was contrary to natural right. . . Now all acts of legislature apparently contrary to natural right and justice, are, in our laws,

[3] "Rights of the British Colonies Asserted and Proved," pp. 41, 47.

and must be in the nature of things, considered as void. The laws of nature are the laws of God; whose authority can be superseded by no power on earth. A legislature must not obstruct our obedience to him from whose punishments they cannot protect us. All human constitutions which contradict his laws, we are in conscience bound to disobey.

Bland, on the other side, did not apparently dispute these arguments, but maintained that the system of degrees or grades in society was conformable to the general scheme of the Creator, and that the position of slaves must be filled by some. The decree of the court was that the Act of 1682 had been repealed by an Act of 1705.[4]

When, at length, the Stamp Act was passed, and the colonies burst out in flames of almost revolution, the leaders of the movement eagerly wanted to save their people from absolute control by a nation at three thousand miles' distance, and at the same time they wanted a basis of reason to show the legality of their course. It was not altogether easy then,—far less so than it seems to us to-day, one hundred and fifty years later,—to find this, and they groped about a good deal for a time in rather a vague way. The beginnings of all principles are vague and groping, and it does not argue against the soundness of our American Doctrine of Judicial Power that it was slowly led up to by halting and uncertain steps, by some backing and filling, by the assertion of alleged principles which will not bear scrutiny.

[4] Robin *v.* Hardaway, Jefferson's (Virginia) Reports, p. 109.

The Courts in Massachusetts were closed after the passage of the Stamp Act, because of its requirement that only stamped paper should be used, and because there were no stamps in the colony.   In this state of circumstances, Boston adopted a petition to the governor and council to open the courts, despite this defect, and the young John Adams found himself suddenly appointed one of the counsel to present the petition.   It was a responsible position for a man of thirty to fill, and Adams was evidently in much doubt as to the best line of argument to adopt.   To quote from his "Diary":

Shall we contend that the Stamp Act is void,—that the Parliament have no authority to impose internal taxes upon us, because we are not represented in it,—and therefore that the Stamp Act ought to be waived by the judges as against natural equity and the constitution?   Shall we use these as arguments for opening the courts of law? Or shall we ground ourselves on necessity only?[5]

He was still a little drifting, too, at the argument, for the same "Diary"[6] has it that he based himself on such contentions as that "the act of law never doth wrong," "An Act of Parliament can do no wrong"; though he did advance the doctrine of Coke, and argue specifically that "Acts of Parliament against reason or impossible to be performed, shall be judged void." A more inspiring outline of his address, but quite con-

[5] John Adams's "Life and Works," Vol. I, pp. 76, 77.
[6] *Ibid.,* Vol. II, pp. 157 *et seq.*

sistent with the foregoing, is to be found in another place. Here he is represented to have spoken thus :[7]

The Stamp Act, I take it, is utterly void, and of no binding force upon us; for it is against our rights as Men and our Privileges as Englishmen. An Act made in defiance of the first Principles of Justice, an Act which rips up the Foundation of the British Constitution and makes void Maxims of eighteen hundred Years' standing.

Parliament may err; they are not infallible; they have been refused to be submitted to. An Act making the King's Proclamation to be law, the Executive Power adjudged absolutely void.

The Stamp Act was made where we are in no sense represented, therefore no more binding upon us, than an Act which should oblige us to destroy One-half of our species.

There are certain Principles fixed unalterably in Nature.

If there was early mist, and if counsel groped in the preparation of the case and even in its argument, much of this was cleared away by the glare of argument, and,—with even a remarkable approach to our modern viewpoint,—the Governor said, after the discussion was over:

The arguments made use of, both by Mr. Adams and you [Otis] would be very pertinent to induce the Judges

[7] Andrew C. McLaughlin's "The Courts, the Constitution and the People," p. 80, citing Justice Gray's article in Quincy's (Mass.) Reports, pp. 200, 201.

of the Superior Court to think the Act of no validity,
and that therefore they should pay no Regard to it; but
the Question with me is whether that very Thing don't
argue the Impropriety of our Intermeddling in a Matter
which solely belongs to them to judge of in their Judicial
Department.[8]

Again, in the matter of the Stamp Act, proceedings
of a similar nature to those in Massachusetts occurred
in Virginia. In the Court of Hustings for Northampton County, so the original minutes of the Court still
record, on February 11, 1766, the Clerk and other
Officers came in and prayed the opinion of the Court
whether the Stamp Act

was binding on the inhabitants of this Colony, and
whether they the said Officers should incur any Penal-
ties by not using Stamp Paper agreeable to the directions of the said Act: The Court unanimously declared
it to be their Opinion that the said Act did not bind,
affect or concern the Inhabitants of this Colony; inasmuch as they conceive the said Act to be unconstitutional.[9]

It was a bold announcement for a Court of minor
jurisdiction to make, and the fact that such a Court

[8] Justice Gray's article in Quincy's (Mass.) Reports, p. 206,
and *see* 204, cited in McLaughlin's "The Courts," etc., p. 81.
[9] McMaster's "United States," Vol. V, pp. 394, 395. Prof. Mc-
Master found this incident in a newspaper of the period and
then traced it to its source. He kindly gave me his results, and
I have secured, as he did, a certified copy of the minute in question, which is contained in "Minute Book No. 27" (1765-71),
p. 30, still preserved among the records of the Court at East-
ville, the capital of Northampton County. The quotation in the
text is from this source.

announced the opinion that the Act was "unconstitutional" seems to show that American opinion was deeply infiltrated with this view.

Revolution and rebellion, the determination to escape in one way or another from the Stamp Act and the absolute control it portended, were of course in the air of the colonies at this time, but it cannot be doubted that the people among whom these opinions were held and this judicial announcement was made, were already far along on the road towards our modern doctrine upon the subject. Otherwise, the Executive in Massachusetts would not possibly have suggested (as it has been seen that it did) that the Judiciary had the express function of examining into the validity of Acts of Parliament, or that in a proper case they "should pay no regard to them."

So far had the belief of the colonists in the doctrine of Lord Coke infiltrated itself among them, that in 1765 Hutchinson summed the matter up by saying with reference to the Stamp Act:

The prevailing reason at this time is that the Act of Parliament is against Magna Charta, and the natural Rights of Englishmen, and therefore, according to Lord Coke, null and void.

And a writer of fame, who examined this whole subject some years ago, wrote that

even the judges appointed by the Royal Governor do not seem to have been prepared to deny this principle. John Cushing, one of the associate Justices, in a letter to Chief Justice Hutchinson, dated "In a hurry, Feby. 7, 1766," upon the question whether the courts should be opened without stamps, wrote, "It's true it is said an Act of Parliament against natural Equity is void. It will be disputed whether this is such an Act. It seems to me the main Question here is whether an Act which cannot be carried into execution should stop the Course of Justice, and that the Judges are more confined than with respect to an obsolete Act." . . . And in 1776, after the Governor had left, and the Council and House of Representatives had assumed the Government, John Adams, in answering a letter of congratulation upon his appointment as Chief Justice of Massachusetts, from Wm. Cushing, his senior associate, and who upon Adams's declination became Chief Justice in his stead, and afterwards a Justice of the Supreme Court of the United States, wrote, "You have my hearty concurrence in telling the jury the nullity of Acts of Parliament." [10]

Nor was this doctrine of Coke's by any means such an extravagance in that day as it doubtless now seems to nearly all of us.[11] As has been pointed

[10] Justice Gray's article on "Writs of Assistance," in Quincy's Reports, Appendix I, pp. 527, 528. Cushing had written Adams, "I can tell the grand jury the nullity of acts of parliament, but must leave you to prove it by the more powerful arguments of the *jus gladii divinum,* a power not peculiar to kings or ministers." To this the ever doughty Adams replied, "You have my hearty concurrence in telling the jury the nullity of acts of parliament, whether we can prove it by the *jus gladii* or not. I am determined to die of that opinion, let the *jus gladii* say what it will." John Adams's "Works," Vol. IX, pp. 390, 391.

[11] Perhaps some approval of Coke's Doctrine is to be found in the "Report of the New York State Bar Association Committee," pp. 15-18. If so, I think few will agree with its view.

out,[12] there was then no little authority for it, and the theory of the omnipotence of Parliament had not yet assumed positive shape. Several judicial decisions had followed rather in the line of Bonham's Case, and Bacon's and Viner's Abridgments, and Comyns' Digest, all leading authorities of about the middle of the eighteenth century, lent their united voices to its support. So the colonists had some ground to stand on, and probably they had chosen the most available weapon of defense they could find.

The long war followed shortly on these events, bringing in its train terrible disorganization, and showing to our public men, even more plainly than to the outside world, the utter nakedness of our system of government. The Central Power could rarely enforce its policy, and had at times to proclaim aloud its incapacity and to call upon the States to enact laws, which it had not the authority to pass or to enforce. The thirteen States,—discordant, dissevered, and not so very far from belligerent,—scorned requisitions, passed laws in the teeth of those of Congress, violated all agreements with foreign powers, and thus plunged our foreign relations into such a condition of conflict and veritable chaos as could not be permitted to continue.

We shall see how all this influenced our public men and helped to drive a much hesitating people, jealous to a degree of one another, and fearful of power, to the creation of a Union which has resulted, for good

[12] Justice Gray's article on "Writs of Assistance," in Quincy's (Mass.) Reports, Appendix I, pp. 395-540, or see New York "Bar Association Committee's Report," immediately above.

or ill, in that very increase of the central power which many of them so dreaded. Could 1787-1788 have foreseen 1915-1918, I think the student of the earlier time will agree that the Constitution would never have been adopted. But this is quite aside from the matters we are concerned with here.

The point for us is how the chaos of war and the lamentable breaking down of our system of administration called aloud for a cure, for some device by which the fourteen wrangling systems of government could be controlled and turned in one direction, which should represent the will of united America. This was fairly burned into the minds of many of our statesmen; and we shall see how it came constantly to the surface in the Convention of 1787,—as well as, in reality, called it into being.

CHAPTER IV

OUR FIRST ACTUAL JUDICIAL DECISIONS THAT LAWS
VIOLATED THE CONSTITUTION AND WERE HENCE
TO BE HELD VOID. RECOGNITION OF THIS DOC-
TRINE. ITS RAPID SPREAD

THE time and the circumstances of 1776-1787
were far from propitious for the creation of desirable
principles of administration; and it is a striking fact
that even during those troublous years the old inherited doctrines of our colonial days, of which preceding pages of this book have treated, still found
expression,—even grew. Heredity continued to assert itself, and selection and specialization of the best
traits of the earlier period began to lead rapidly
towards that system of Judicial Power, which the
United States have ever known.

To this period belong the first actual decisions of
our courts that specific laws passed by the Legislature
were unauthorized, and hence void, or unconstitutional,
and the court's consequent refusal to enforce them;
while in other cases, or in other bodies, the general
doctrine was recognized and at times most boldly asserted by men of prominence, if in some instances the
assertion was hesitating, or perhaps even vague.
Many a rill and many a rivulet was flowing slowly on

to unite at length in that vast river that has ever characterized the American Judicial System.

In that period, the first instance in which the subject was possibly discussed and considered was the case of Josiah Philips in Virginia in 1778-79; but it furnishes no precedent [1] and is only to be noted because it has long been thought to be one, and because the contradictory statements of the various actors in it at a much later period,—when waning memory was failing them, with all other faculties,—have always seemed to indicate that the question of the court's power to decline to carry out a law, on the ground of its unconstitutionality, was at least talked of in the consideration of the case. But, as shown above, late investigation has demonstrated that the question was in reality never presented by the facts of the case and the utterly irreconcilable old-man statements of the

[1] Philips had long hidden in the swamps of Virginia, coming out now and then to devastate and maraud. The authorities could not apprehend him, and finally the Legislature, on motion of Jefferson, passed an act of attainder against him in May, 1778, to go into effect if he should not give himself up by June 30, 1778. He was later tried for robbery and executed, but it has until recently been a matter of doubt whether this was because the Attorney-General decided not to act upon the attainder or because the court held the attainder unconstitutional. The various statements of the chief actors and of historians cannot be reconciled. It has been recently shown, however, by Jesse Turner ("A Phantom Precedent," in *Amer. Law Review*, Vol. XLVIII, pp. 321-344), from a record of Princess Ann County, that on June 11, 1778 (before the attainder was to come into being), Philips was present in court and was charged with feloniously robbing. See also Edward S. Corwin's "Doctrine of Judicial Review," pp. 71, 72: Burk's Girardin's "Virginia," Vol. IV, pp. 305, 306; Tucker's "Blackstone," Vol. I, Appendix, p. 293: "The Case of Josiah Philips," by Wm. P. Trent, *Amer. Histor. Rev.*, Vol. I, pp. 444-54; *etc., etc.*

actors in it are far too vague to furnish a foundation for history.

The march of time brings us now almost suddenly to the first well-established case in our country, in which a court undertook to decide that a specific statute passed by their Legislature was in violation of the Constitution, and hence void, and that the court would for this reason decline to carry it into execution.

In 1778 the Legislature of New Jersey had passed an act providing for the seizure of goods belonging to the enemy, and directing that the trial in such cases should be held by a jury of six, from whose decision there should be no appeal. It was a violent law, but was passed to meet a great and trying evil. There was at the time a specific provision in the New Jersey Constitution that "the inestimable right of trial by jury shall remain confirmed as a part of the law of this colony, without repeal forever," and there were other pertinent provisions of her earliest laws, one of which read that "the trial of all causes . . . shall be heard and decided by the verdict or judgment of twelve honest men."

Proceeding under the Act of 1778, Walton, an army officer, seized goods in the possession of Holmes,[2]

[2] All the facts stated in the text in regard to Holmes *v.* Walton, unless otherwise specified, are taken from President Austin Scott's "Holmes *v.* Walton, The New Jersey Precedent," "Rutgers College Publications, No. 8," reprinted from *Amer. Histor. Review*, Vol. IV (April, 1899). Holmes *v.* Walton is referred to in State *v.* Parkhurst, 4 Halstead, 444, and at the time of my article of 1885 I knew of it only from this source, and drew some erroneous conclusions. President Scott has since identified the case and shown these errors.

as belonging to an enemy; and the judgment having gone against Holmes, after trial before a jury of six, Holmes took out a *certiorari* to remove the record to the Supreme Court of the State. The case was argued before the Supreme Court in November, 1779, but was not decided until September, 1780, when the court unanimously reversed the decree of the court below, evidently for the reason that the Act of 1778 authorizing a jury of six was held to violate the Constitution of the State, and hence to be void.

The opinion has not survived, but collateral matters make it plain that this was the reason of the court's decision,[3] and the Legislature recognized in effect the propriety of the decision, by passing a new statute in the matter, requiring a jury of twelve on the demand of either side. Holmes *v.* Walton was decided by David Brearly,[4] the Chief Justice of the State, and at the same time William Paterson was Attorney-General, and William Livingston Governor and also Chancellor. We shall see later the part these three men took in the Federal Convention of 1787,

[3] "The New Jersey Precedent," pp. 7, 8. For example, shortly after the decision citizens presented a petition to the House, complaining that "the Justices of the Supreme Court have set aside some of the laws as unconstitutional, and made void the proceedings of the magistrates, though strictly agreeable to the said laws." Again, at a later stage of Holmes *v.* Walton, counsel assumed in argument that "a trial by six men is unconstitutional."

[4] His colleagues on the bench were Smith and Symmes. All three members of the Court had served in the field, and yet agreed in the decision, despite the urgency of the evil which the Act was intended to stop. William Willcocks was originally counsel for the winning party, and Elias Boudinot also appeared for him later.

and the use they seem to have made of Holmes *v.* Walton.

Gouverneur Morris, too, knew of the decision,—at least, a very few years after its date, and Varnum,—soon of Trevett *v.* Weeden fame,—was a member of Congress, was present in Philadelphia at the time of the decision, and almost certain to have heard of such a case decided on the other side of the Delaware, which was then a matter of controversy in New Jersey, and of course argued among public men generally.[5]

Commonwealth *v.* Caton[6] in the Court of Appeals of Virginia in 1782 is the next case for us to consider in point of time. This case is not one where any law was held to be unconstitutional, but the general question was under consideration by the court, and the case is particularly noteworthy on account of the clearness and great boldness with which members of the bench announced their right and power to decline to carry out a law, on the ground of its unconstitutionality. It is hence not a lawyer's precedent, and the remarks of the judges were *obiter dicta;* but history does not confine its consideration to such narrow and technical rules. In its domain, the fact that leading men held and boldly announced certain views, under great responsibility, is most persuasive evidence that those views rested on some solid foundation and were tending to be accepted of the sons of men.

The questions presented by Comm. *v.* Caton were

[5] "The New Jersey Precedent," as above.
[6] 4 Call, p. 5.

two: (1) Whether an Act of the Virginia Legislature of 1776,—defining treason, and under which the prisoners had been convicted,—was a violation of the State Constitution, and (2) Whether, under the Virginia Constitution, a pardon of the prisoners by a vote of the House of Burgesses alone was valid. The Court held that the Act of 1776 did not infringe the State Constitution, and that the pardon by the Burgesses alone was not valid; but then the members of the Court went on to announce their views upon the general question, and were most of them very clear as to their power and duty to hold a statute unconstitutional in a proper case. Wythe, J., said:

Nay, more, if the whole Legislature, an event to be deprecated, should attempt to overleap the bounds prescribed to them by the people, I, in administering the public justice of the country, will meet the united powers at my seat in this tribunal and, pointing to the constitution, will say to them, here is the limit of your authority, and hither shall you go, but no further.

The report adds that

Chancellor Blair and the rest of the judges were of opinion that the court had power to declare any resolution or act of the Legislature, or of either branch of it, to be unconstitutional and void,

while the note of doubt, which was to be expected, and which shows that the vast import of the question was not lost sight of, was sounded by Pendleton, J., who said:

But how far this court, in whom the judicial powers may in some sort be said to be concentrated, shall have the power to declare the nullity of a law passed in its forms by the legislative powers without exercising the powers of that branch, contrary to the plain terms of that Constitution, is, indeed, a deep, important, and I will add, tremendous, question, the decision of which might involve consequences to which gentlemen may not have extended their ideas.[7]

An instance occurred in Pennsylvania in 1782, which is, however, no judicial decision upon the subject, and did not even reach the courts, but which curiously illustrates how the same ferment was working in the minds of Americans generally and, when it is coupled with the instance next to be mentioned in that same leading State, shows how widespread was the conviction of the judicial function in the matter of unconstitutional laws.

During the war Washington had given a passport to a British officer to transport clothing to British prisoners at Lancaster, and a large quantity of goods had accordingly been conveyed into the State for that

[7] Pendleton was apparently still a little in doubt at the time of the Virginia Ratifying Convention some six years later, and said: "My brethren in that department [the judicial] felt great uneasiness in their minds to violate the Constitution by such a law. They have prevented the operation of some unconstitutional laws. Notwithstanding those violations, I rely upon the principles of government—that it will produce its own reform, by the responsibility resulting from frequent elections." Cited from Elliot's "Debates," Vol. III, p. 299, in Horace A. Davis's "The Annulment of Legislation by the Supreme Court," in *Amer. Polit. Sci. Rev.*, Vol. VII, p. 573.

purpose.   As this was directly against an express law of the State, the goods

were seized and condemned by the proper magistrate. On a complaint to the Legislature of the State, they referred the same to their judicial officers, upon whose report (that Congress being vested with the power of declaring war, the right of giving safe passports to an enemy was necessarily implied, which, therefore, was duly exercised by their Commander-in-Chief, though no express power was given to him for that purpose) the Legislature declared their law directing the condemnation of the goods void *ab initio,* and the judgment of condemnation had no effect.[8]

In the pinch of doubt, the Legislature called upon "their judicial officers" to resolve for them the question of the propriety, or even validity, of a statute of the State, and on their report declared the law void.

The opinions held in Pennsylvania appear still more clearly in another instance.   That State's Constitution

[8] Frank E. Melvin's "The Judicial Bulwark of the Constitution," *Amer. Polit. Sci. Rev.,* Vol. VIII, pp. 167-204: see especially p. 194.   Mr. Melvin has not yet, I think, published in full his evidence in regard to this case, but he shows that the instance is referred to in "Annals of Congress, First Congress," p. 1925, and the details in my text are taken from there.   The statute of Pennsylvania regulating the importation was passed September 20, 1782, and is to be found in "Statutes at Large of Pennsylvania," Vol. X, pp. 497-505, and its partial repeal of March 20, 1783, in *ibid.,* Vol. XI, pp. 68-70.   The repealing statute recites the provisions of the original act requiring the nature and quantity of clothing intended for prisoners of war to be certified to the President and Council of the State before importation, and then goes on: "And whereas such provision is deemed contrary to [the spirit of] the 9th article of the Confederation," etc., etc., that therefore that portion of the act is hereby made void and repealed.   The Ninth Article of the Confederation conferred on Congress the power to declare war.

of 1776 provided for a Council of Censors, whose duty it was, among other things, "to inquire whether the Constitution has been preserved inviolate in every part," etc., etc. This Council met in November, 1783, and appointed a committee to inquire what parts of the Constitution required amendment and whether the instrument had been preserved inviolate. The Committee reported in January, 1784, that there had been numerous deviations from the Constitution which they regarded as infringements, as well as suggested parts which they thought defective. In this latter connection, they wrote that by the Constitution,

the judges of the Supreme Court are to be commissioned for seven years only and are removable (for misbehavior) at any time, by the general assembly. Your committee conceive the said constitution to be in this respect materially defective . . .

Because (2), if the assembly should pass an unconstitutional law, *and the judges have virtue enough to refuse to obey it,* the same assembly could instantly remove them.

The report was adopted.[9]

Rutgers *v.* Waddington, decided in New York in 1784, is the next case in the history of this matter; and it is a highly important one, owing to the burning

[9] "The Proceedings relative to the calling of the Conventions of 1776 and 1790, etc., etc., and the Council of Censors" (Harrisburg, 1825), pp. 66, 67, 69, 70-114: I am indebted to E. S. Corwin's "Doctrine of Judicial Review," pp. 40, 41, for this instance. See L. H. Meader on the "Pennsylvania Council of Censors," in *Pennsylvania Magazine of History and Biography* for October, 1898. The italics in the text above are mine.

public interest at the time in regard to the decision, though it did not turn, as did the other cases treated in this chapter, upon an incompatibility between a State statute and the fundamental law of the same State, but between a State statute and an authorized action of the Central Government. This distinction seems to have escaped observation at the time, and the case appears to have been regarded by opponents precisely as were the others here considered, merely from the general standpoint that the Judiciary was arrogating powers to itself; nevertheless, the difference is in reality very great, and the case will be best treated in the next chapter, together with some others of a like character.

The year 1785 was marked by the Symsbury case [10] in Connecticut, which was an ejectment by the town of Symsbury demanding the surrender of certain ground, held by the defendant Bidwell under a conveyance by New Hartford. The original grant to Symsbury, made in 1670, had been contended by newer and rival towns not to be clear as to its extent, and a committee had been appointed by the General Assembly, without the concurrence of Symsbury, to make a survey and lay out the lines. This was done, and the report confirmed by the Assembly, with the result that the lands in suit were found to be outside the grant to Symsbury.

But the court, in the suit of 1785, was of opinion that this was an error, that the original grant to Symsbury had contained the lands in question and that

[10] Kirby's Reports, pp. 444-453.

the title was still in that town, unless otherwise divested. They had never agreed to the survey, and the court was hence of opinion that

the Act of the General Assembly, confirming Kimberley's [the surveyor's] line, operated to restrict and limit . . . the jurisdiction of the town of Symsbury, but could not legally operate to curtail the land before granted to the proprietors of the town of Symsbury, without their consent,

and that their grant being the prior one, the title was in them. Judgment was accordingly entered for the plaintiff. The case was merely in the County Court of Litchfield, but the judge writes that the same point had been decided by them in the same way the year before, and that their ruling had been affirmed by the Supreme Court of Errors.

Symsbury's case was certainly in a technical sense a clear decision in point, but it seems to have been entirely wanting in that eager and burning attention on the part of the bar and the public which marked some of the other cases at about the same date. But, even if it was thus less educative, it serves,—perhaps even more plainly,—to show how the doctrine was silently spreading far and wide, and coming to be accepted by the bench and bar. Even a dissenting judge in a like case in error wrote:[11]

I think it ought to be admitted in the case before us, that the proprietors of Symsbury could not have their

[11] *Ibid.*, pp. 448-453.

grant taken from them, or curtailed, even by the General Assembly, without their consent.

Trevett *v*. Weeden, in Rhode Island in 1786, is another case in which a State statute was squarely held unconstitutional, and was refused enforcement because of being in conflict with a higher, fundamental law.[12]

Rhode Island had issued a large amount of paper money, and had provided that, in case a tender of it should be refused, a heavy penalty might be recovered against the party refusing, and that the trial of such a case should be held without a jury. The fundamental law, on the other hand, preserved inviolate the ancient right of trial by jury. Trevett *v*. Weeden presented the issue here involved, excited intense interest with the public, and was argued at length. Varnum for the defendant quoted in his argument from Locke and Vattel, adapting their abstract views of infant society and social compact to the actual history of towns in Rhode Island. He cited a passage from Vattel to the effect that the Legislature cannot alter the fundamental constitutional law, without express authority so to do, and ending "In short, these legislators derive their power from the constitution; how then can they change it, without destroying the foun-

[12] Brinton Coxe ("Judicial Power and Unconstitutional Legislation," p. 267) and some other writers distinguish Trevett *v*. Weeden on the ground that Rhode Island had then no written constitution, but the Colonial charter had been at least tacitly recognized as their fundamental law, and the statute in question was distinctly held to violate the provisions of that charter or constitution.

dation of their authority?"[13]—words to be found in American history often since. The Court held the statute unconstitutional, but the judges were then summoned to appear before the Legislature and explain their decision. They were appointed annually by the Assembly, and were not reëlected at the ensuing election.

The case is the first, but far from the last, in which a contest was made over the right claimed by the judiciary, and the great excitement in regard to the decisions in this particular case and in Rutgers *v.* Waddington, seems to exclude absolutely as to them at least the belief held by some writers, that in those days even important decisions remained unknown for long periods or forever. The great interest of the body of lawyers, the public meetings and agitation by the mass of the people and in the legislative halls, were far too great for such a result to follow.

Nor is this all. It is not the way of lawyers, in the flush of a great victory, to hide their light under a bushel. Varnum, the winning counsel in Trevett *v.* Weeden, was a man widely known, then (1786-1787), as well as in 1780-1782, a member of Congress, and so little was he silent in regard to his success that he almost at once (1787) published quite a pamphlet,[14] which went at length into the case and his argument.

Rutgers *v.* Waddington, as will be seen, had also been the subject of a contemporary pamphlet. Pam-

[13] Coxe's "Judicial Power," etc., p. 240.
[14] "The Case of Trevett *v.* Weeden," by J. M. Varnum; also *see* McMaster's "United States," Vol. I, pp. 337-339, and Coxe's "Judicial Power," etc., pp. 234-248.

phlets are written for the very purpose of making a subject known, and exclude the idea of oblivion. As to Varnum, it is, I submit, impossible to conceive that he,—who, we are told,[15] was recognized by his colleagues in Congress as "a man of uncommon talents and most brilliant eloquence,"—did otherwise than talk and perhaps even boast of his triumph, as well as circulate his pamphlet, so that his then colleagues in Congress, and many other leading men, must quickly have become aware that at least in Trevett *v.* Weeden it had been judicially held that an Act of Assembly was in violation of the State Constitution, and that the Court had for this reason declined to enforce the act.

Perhaps, too, as has been already hinted in these pages, Varnum had in turn derived his inspiration from Holmes *v.* Walton, which had been decided while he was a member of Congress (1780-82) and in Philadelphia, necessarily in close touch with many of the leading men of the country. And whether this conjecture,—for such, of course, it is,—as to the knowledge of Holmes *v.* Walton by Varnum and thinking public men is justified or not, that case was at least well known to Gouverneur Morris in 1785,[16] while Trevett *v.* Weeden,—evidently without search in regard to this special point,—has been found reported in five contemporary newspapers.[17]

[15] Appleton's Dictionary, *sub* Varnum.
[16] Austin Scott's "The New Jersey Precedent," p. 12, citing Sparks's "Life of Gouverneur Morris," Vol. III, p. 438.
[17] Coxe's "Judicial Power," etc., p. 247, citing McMaster's "United States," Vol. I, p. 339. See, also, Coxe, pp. 234-248.

Rutgers *v.* Waddington, too, which was decided in 1784,—and which is treated in the next Chapter,— excited intense interest in New York, and knowledge of the case traveled far and wide. Not only was it noticed at some length in a newspaper published on June 17, 1785, as far away as Charleston, but this paper's article was reprinted in the *Pennsylvania Gazette* of July 13, 1785, from which publication we learn that the Mayor, who had decided the case,

having a high opinion of Lord Mansfield's wisdom and impartiality, drew up a clear statement of the case, and desired to know his opinion, whether the law of nations did not sanction the distinctions made in the judgment delivered by the Mayor's Court of New York. Lord Mansfield has sent back an answer, expressed in terms of the greatest politeness to the Mayor, informing him, that, in his opinion, the law of nations could never be pleaded against a law of the land.

Trevett *v.* Weeden and Rutgers *v.* Waddington, at least, were certainly not allowed to fall into oblivion; and we shall find the same to have been the case as to Bayard *v.* Singleton in 1787.

The principle involved in the foregoing cases was also known and recognized in New Hampshire in 1785-87. William Plumer, a leading lawyer of the State, who often met Jeremiah Mason and Daniel Webster in forensic battle at the famous Rockingham County bar, was a member of the Legislature of the State in 1785, and wrote that at the second session held in that year:

I entered my protest singly and alone, against the bill for the recovery of small debts in an expeditious way and manner; *principally on the ground that it was unconstitutional. The courts so pronounced it, and the succeeding legislature repealed the law.*[18]

Here is, of course, no judicial decision, but a most positive statement of the general doctrine in the Legislature, and an apparent recognition of it by the Legislature itself. What makes this instance,—and, still more, the case of McClary *v.* Gilman, referred tó *infra,*[19]—very noteworthy is the fact that a pet fancy of the New Hampshire Legislature of colonial times had been to interfere with judicial proceedings, especially by passing a bill to grant a new trial to a suitor

[18] "The Life of William Plumer" by his son William Plumer, Jr., p. 59. Italics are mine. I have secured from the office of the Secretary of State of New Hampshire copies of the Act of November 9, 1785, "for the recovery of small debts in an expeditious way and manner," and of that of June 28, 1787, repealing "an Act passed the ninth day of November, 1785, entitled" as immediately above. The laws are in manuscript, that of 1785 in Vol. V, pp. 147-149, and that of 1787 in *ibid.,* p. 367. Plumer apparently meant that the courts pronounced the particular act unconstitutional, but his memory perhaps deceived him here, and at least the first known judicial decision seems to have been rendered in a case of his in 1791, as will appear later. His biographer, however states ("Life," pp. 170-172) that this case of 1791 (McClary *v.* Gilman, *infra* pp. 173, 174) was not the first case in which a law was held unconstitutional. Plumer was not mistaken in regard to the *repeal* of the Act of 1785, as is shown by the citation from the legislative records. Jeremiah Mason was also (as Mr. F. E. Melvin (*Amer. Polit. Sci. Rev.,* Vol. VIII, p. 194) has pointed out) counsel in another county of New Hampshire,—Westmoreland,—in similar cases where the Legislature had been guilty of "prescribing special rules for the trial of a particular action" at approximately the same date. "Memoir of Jeremiah Mason," pp. 26, 27.

[19] Pp. 173, 174.

who had lost his case: "restoring a party to his rights," as it was called. Numerous such laws of the colony had been disallowed by the Crown in Council; and at one time, in 1764, no less than sixteen "extraordinary" laws were so brought to naught, the representation for their repeal reading:

> The practice of passing laws of this nature . . . is of such a dangerous tendency and example, and many of the laws are so unconstitutional and unjust that we fear it will be necessary that your Majesty's disallowance of them should be made public in order to deter the Legislatures of your Majesty's colonies from assuming powers and taking cognizance of matters that do constitutionally belong to the Courts of Justice alone.

The evil habit of passing such laws continued after independence,[20] and soon led, as will be later shown, to plain judicial decisions that such laws were void.

Finally, one other indication of how widespread was the belief in the power of the Judiciary in regard to unconstitutional laws must be mentioned. This instance has not to do with a decision of a court, or even the expressed opinion of any governmental agency, nor did it happen at a great center of thought,

[20] Plumer's "Plumer," pp. 170-172. I have considered this long line of New Hampshire precedents in my article "The American Doctrine of Judicial Power, and Its Early Origin," in 47 *Amer. Law Review,* pp. 684-688, and have there stated how much I was indebted in the matter to the aid of the late Albert S. Batchellor, the well-known editor of the New Hampshire State Papers. See his "New Hampshire Provincial Papers," Vol. VII, pp. 2, 199, 200, 221, and his introduction to Vol. I of the "New Hampshire Laws," pp. 49, 50, 520, 710, 859-879. See also Oliver M. Dickerson's "Colonial Government," p. 273 and generally.

where new ideas, good and bad, are most likely to find expression, but in the very fact of its occurrence in an outlying district,—among a number of young men whose lives still lay before them, and some of whom later had careers of distinction,—is to be found the strongest proof of the sturdy growth by this date of the American Doctrine of Judicial Power.

In Danville, Kentucky, there existed from 1786 to 1790 a debating club which called itself "The Political Club." The very existence of the society was forgotten in Kentucky history until late in the following century some of its records were found [21] by chance among old family papers. Among the club's members,—thirty in number,—was George ·Muter, Chief Justice of the District Court of Kentucky at the time of the Club's formation in 1786, and a member of the Court of Appeals from 1792 until after 1801, at which date he was Chief Justice.

In this latter year (1801), in Stidger v. Rogers,[22] the Court of Appeals held that a State statute was in violation of their constitution, hence void; and they were inclined to think that the same statute changed the obligation of a contract, and thereby violated the

---

[21] By Thomas Speed, who afterwards edited them in "The Political Club, Danville, Ky., 1786-1790" ("Filson Club Publications, No. 9, 1894"). I am indebted to T. L. Edelen, Esq., of the bar of Frankfort, Ky., for calling my attention to this instance, and also to Mr. Alfred Pirtle of Louisville, Ky., the present editor of the Filson Club, and to Miss Mary W. Speed of Louisville, Ky., the present owner of the papers in question, for aid in tracing out the Club's doings. My account of the matter is of course taken from the publication mentioned above, except where otherwise specified.

[22] Kentucky Decisions, p. 64.

Federal Constitution as well. We shall soon see how the Chief Justice may have at least been influenced in this matter by some discussions of the Political Club. Another member of the Club was Thomas Todd, who was appointed to the Court of Appeals in the very end of 1801, and had a hand in some of the similar decisions soon following on Stidger *v.* Rogers.

Still others "conspicuous in shaping the beginnings of Kentucky,"—members of constitutional conventions and so on,—were members of the Club, and with the ardor and exuberance of youth, they discussed many a knotty problem. Slavery and the slave-trade, the proposed United States Constitution, suffrage, the form of government for Kentucky, whether there should be one or two branches of the Legislature, the powers of the second branch,—all these immense questions were debated by the Club, and on no less than two occasions they discussed the very problem we are concerned with: of statutes violating the Constitution, and of what it was in such a case the duty of a court to do.

The only reference to the Club's existence, apart from its long-lost records, seems to be contained in the "Diary" of Major Beatty, a paymaster in the United States Army, who spent the night at Danville on April 29, 1787,[23] and wrote in his "Diary" that he had been much disturbed by

[23] The Filson Club publication gives this date as August 29, 1786, but Miss Speed called my attention to the fact that there is certainly an error here, as the Club did not hold its first meeting until December 27, 1786. After some correspondence, I found that the original "Diary" is preserved in the Collections

a Political Club which met in the room next where we slept and kept us awake until 12 or 1 o'clock. . . . The dispute was: One side insisted that an "Act of Assembly was no law when it did not perfectly agree with the Constitution of the State." It was opposed by the other party, and a very long debate took place. To which the editor of the papers adds that the minutes of the club contain an account of this very debate, and show that the decision of the club was that an Act of Assembly must be in accordance with the Constitution of the State.

Apparently, this moot point was a favorite one with the members, for again on May 5, 1787, they discussed the question: "If an Act of Assembly should be contrary to the Constitution, which ought to govern a judge in his decision?", and after the debate it was resolved: "as the opinion of the club that when an Act of Assembly is contrary to the Constitution, the judge ought to govern his decision by the Constitution."

Todd, who later had a share in the early Kentucky decisions upon this subject, and who was appointed in 1807 a Justice of the Supreme Court of the United States, was the President of The Political Club during the evening of May 5, 1787.

It seems impossible to understand the occurrence of these discussions among a lot of youths in an out-

of the New York Historical Society, and Mr. Kelby, the Librarian, kindly corrected the error for me. He also informed me that the "Diary" has been published in the "Magazine of American History," Vol. I, pp. 175-179, 235-243, 309-315, 380-384, 432-438. This publication has the incident in question noted under April 29, 1787.

lying district, far from the swarming hives of men, unless the thesis which they were debating was already full-high advanced among their countrymen at some of the great centers, and had thence filtered out to a considerable number of public men far and wide throughout the country.

CHAPTER V

RUTGERS *v.* WADDINGTON. OTHER LIKE CASES IN
STATE COURTS HOLDING VOID STATE STATUTES IN
CONFLICT WITH FEDERAL ACTION. CONGRESS
URGES THE GENERAL USE OF THE JUDICIAL DE-
PARTMENT TO ANNUL SUCH LAWS OF THE STATES

DURING the same period in which were decided the
cases we have been considering, from about the end of
the war to the meeting of the Federal Convention, occurred other matters of vast influence upon the chapter
of American history with which this book is concerned.
It was a time of drifting and disorganization, with a
number of small and very new States or Nations,—
for such they then were,—legislating in many harmful
ways, while the Central Government was barely able
to keep itself alive and to appease the wrath of other
countries. These years have, not inaptly, been called
by a well-known writer "The Critical Period."

Hosts of laws were passed by the States, which led
to imbroglios at home or abroad, but the ones which
chiefly concern us here,—because (as will shortly be
seen) they inevitably drove America still further on
the road towards her doctrine of Judicial Power,—
were those which violated treaties made with foreign
countries, particularly the Treaty of Peace.

Laws in contravention of the Treaty of Peace with Great Britain,—or at least strenuously objected to by the latter Power upon that ground,—existed in nearly all the States, and were a most serious handicap to those who administered our General Government. Thirteen States with popular Legislatures, interspersed of course with time-serving demagogues, whose chief aim in public affairs was to make themselves solid with the masses, and who were often lamentably ignorant of international relations and of the obligations of faith and honor which they carried, were not calculated to lead to a strict adherence to promises made in treaties negotiated by the weak and far-removed Central Power.

America then made a bad name for herself; and the leading men in Congress were often at their wits' end to decide what to do. Knowing well these violations of treaties, often confronted with bitter complaints from foreign countries that prior treaties had been repeatedly deprived by the States of all actual effect, the administrators of our foreign affairs had indeed a hard task. Madison spoke in the Federal Convention of the violations by the States of

the law of nations and of treaties, which, if not prevented, must involve us in the calamities of foreign wars. [And went on] . . . the files of Congress contain complaints already from almost every nation with which treaties have been formed.[1]

[1] Elliot's "Debates," Vol. V, p. 207.

The evil was crying and called aloud for amendment, but there was not power enough vested in the Central Government for it to be able to enforce its wishes. The subject was discussed in Congress, at least as early as 1783, and there can be no doubt that the method of cure was long and often talked of among leading men. It is certainly most noteworthy that the governmental agency finally and knowingly fixed upon by Congress, in order to be certain of getting rid of these unauthorized and unconstitutional laws, was—as we shall later find to have been the case,—the Judiciary.

Before coming to this, however, it will be necessary to consider the case of Rutgers *v.* Waddington and to show what was done in the matter by the Judiciaries in several States, of their own motion. In the first place it must be noted that these cases were not the same in principle as the ones which have been examined in the prior Chapter. All of these latter were concerned with a conflict between a statute and the Constitution of the State itself, to which the Court making the decision also belonged. Those now in hand were instances of a conflict between a State statute and a proceeding of the Central Power, authorized by all the States. The difference is, of course, important, and the existence of this second class of conflicts in our midst was beyond doubt one of the chief causes, which led our ancestors to look to the Judiciary in all such cases. It was absolutely necessary to devise some means by which State laws violating the Federal authority could be quietly set aside, or a General Government was impossible.

Rutgers v. Waddington, which has already been mentioned, was the first case of the kind, and was by far the most conspicuous. It excited intense interest in New York, where it was decided, and, beyond all doubt, knowledge of the decision traveled far and wide. Yet the case does not seem to have been at all distinguished at the time from those in which an incompatibility of a State statute with the Constitution of the same State lay at the bottom of the trouble. The decision of the case presented the gravest difficulties, in that the judgment to be entered might well be one to add fuel to the fire of British dissatisfaction at real and alleged violations by us of the Treaty of Peace.

Rutgers v. Waddington [2] was decided by the Mayor's Court of New York City in 1784. It was an action of trespass, brought under a recent State statute, to recover rent for a brewery, which had been held by the defendant under the orders of the British military leaders (and to whom rent had already been paid), during the occupation by the British. The ground of the decision against the claim was certainly not made very clear by the court, and to the public the main point was that a statute of the Legislature, passed for a very express purpose, was largely frit-

[2] An account of the case was published in 1784 in pamphlet form, and in 1866 this was reprinted, with a valuable "Historical Introduction," by Henry B. Dawson. My text is based entirely on the latter publication, except in the few instances in which I have stated otherwise. See also Coxe's "Judicial Power," etc. pp. 223-233, for another résumé based mainly on Dawson.

tered away by interpretation.   It seems clear that the
more honest course would have been to declare openly
that the statute was no longer valid as to any parts
which conflicted with the terms of the Treaty of
Peace made by Congress in pursuance of its undoubted
powers.   The Court, however, probably obsessed by
the picture distinguished counsel had evidently drawn
of the serious consequences which might follow the
decision of the case, had recourse to what is sometimes
called "the equity of the statute," and strained the
principles of the law in a labored effort to demonstrate
that there was no conflict between the statute and the
Treaty of Peace.   They sought thus to avoid a clash
either of the State with Congress or of the Judiciary
with the State Legislature.

The New York law of March 17, 1783, had been
passed after the British army had sailed for England,
and when impoverished refugee Americans were re-
turning home.   There could be no doubt of the intention of the Legislature; little doubt that the law was
an improper one, and none whatsoever, that, under
the terms of the Treaty of Peace,[3] the State statute
would lead to bitter complaints by the English.   It
authorized in plain words a suit in trespass by any
refugee owner, who had remained an adherent of the
patriot cause, to recover rent from those who had oc-

[3] The provisional treaty had been signed at Paris on November 30, 1782, but the definitive treaty not until September 3, 1783,
—after the passage of the New York Law.   The treaty was ratified by Congress on January 4, 1784.   It contained language by
which any claims of citizens of either country to retribution or
indemnity were released.

cupied his real estate during the possession of the city by the British, and it very specifically provided that "no defendant . . . shall be permitted to plead in justification any military order or command of the enemy."

In reply to the plaintiff's claim, the defendant pleaded that he was "a British subject, a merchant, residing in an enemy's city, under the protection of the British army, by whom it had been conquered," and that on a given date the Commissary General had taken possession of the premises in question "by virtue of authority from the Commander-in-Chief," and that subsequently the defendant had occupied them under a license and permission from the Commissary General, while still later he had held them under a license and permission from the British Commander-in-Chief at a rent of £150 per annum. And he further pleaded that under the Treaty of Peace and according to the general rules of international law, any claim which citizens of either country might have had to retribution or indemnity was relinquished and released. The plaintiff's replication set up the provision of the statute: that no defendant should be allowed to plead any military order in defense. There were then demurrers by both sides.

It is apparent that Rutgers *v.* Waddington presented questions of the utmost seriousness. The Court,—one of very minor jurisdiction, and largely confined to matters of police,—wrote that the case was represented as being of "high importance," because of involving questions which must affect the "national character"; and all this seems to have had its effect, and to have led the judges to seek far and wide for some means of escape from the threatening difficulties.

The case was elaborately argued upon the demurrers on June 29, before "a crowded and attentive auditory," no less than seven counsel being orally heard. The plaintiff was represented by Egbert Benson, the Attorney-General of the State, and three other lawyers, while such great luminaries as Alexander Hamilton, Brockholst Livingston, and Morgan Lewis were all for the defendant. And we need not wonder at this array of counsel, for Rutgers *v.* Waddington seems to have been regarded as a test-case, and many other like ones were either pending or ripe for suit. Hamilton tells us that there was a general opinion, "embracing almost our whole bar, as well as the public," that it was useless to defend against such claims, and he adds that judgments were consequently entered against the defendants in other suits, or compromises made, without serious contest. He alone, he says, took the opposite view "and opposed the Treaty to the Act"; but even after his brilliant (though partial) victory, he so feared the result of a writ of error [4] that Rutgers *v.* Waddington itself and

[4] "Though I was never overruled in the Supreme Court," he wrote, "I never got my point established there. I effected many compromises to [sic] my clients, afraid myself of the event in the Supreme Court, and produced delays until the exceptionable part of the act was repealed. The Supreme Court frequently, in a studied manner, evaded the main question, and turned their decision upon the forms of pleading." Hamilton's "Works," by J. C. Hamilton, Vol. V, pp. 106-137: see especially pp. 115, 116. *Ibid.,* Vol. VII, p. 199.

other like cases in his hands were, under his advice, settled by compromise.

The Mayor, who presided in the Court, was James Duane, a lawyer and a man long distinguished in public affairs.[5] With him sate Richard Varick, the Recorder, and five aldermen. Duane rendered a most elaborate opinion on August 27, but it is so labored that it is no easy task to grasp very definitely what was the ground on which the Court really rested, while a great part of the opinion is hardly to be sustained in law.[6] Much was said of whether the plaintiff's case was within the intent of the statute, and of "whether the Law of Nations gives the captors and Defendant under them rights which control the operation of the statute and bar the present suit"; and, again, of whether the Treaty of Peace implied such an amnesty as to past actions as released the defendant; but the Court relied mainly on its belief that the Law of Nations did give the captors of a hostile city the right to occupy houses and to lease them for strictly military purposes, and interpreted the statute as not meant to include any one acting in pursuance of such right. The opinion reads:

Whoever then is *clearly exempted* from the operation of this statute by the law of nations, this court must take

[5] In 1789, Duane was appointed United States District Judge in New York, and in 1792 was one of the judges to hold the Invalid Pension Act of that year unconstitutional. See *infra*, p. 178.

[6] It has been shown in the preceding chapter (p. 73, *ante*) that Lord Mansfield, when consulted, wrote the Mayor that, in his opinion, the Law of Nations could never be pleaded against a Law of the Land.

it for granted, could never have been *intended* to be comprehended within it by the Legislature.

This interpretation under what is called "the equity of the statute" was the main ground of the decision; but it was in the very teeth of the act, and, beyond doubt, contrary to its most plain intent.

One thing is very evident. Whatever was in reality the actual basis of the decision, no claim was made in words of a right in the Judiciary to question a statute passed by the Legislature. To quote Duane's opinion:

The supremacy of the Legislature need not be called into question; if they think fit positively to enact a law, there is no power which can control them. When the main intent of such a law is clearly expressed, . . . the Judges are not at liberty . . . to reject it: for this were to set the judicial above the legislative which would be subversive of all government.

But when a law is expressed in general words, and some collateral matter, which happens to arise from those general words, is unreasonable, there the judges are in decency to conclude, that the consequences were not foreseen by the legislature; and therefore they are at liberty to expound the statute by equity, and only *quoad hoc* to disregard it.

The principle was undoubtedly sound, but its application by the Court was surely less so. To argue that the question whether this very specific statute applied to the defendant's case was a collateral matter, *happening to arise* under the statute, was carrying interpretation far beyond its utmost limit, for plainly such was the very main purpose of the law, and the statute could otherwise have little to operate upon.[7]

The case did not go by without reference to the doctrine of Coke, which has been so often mentioned in these pages, and which was so popular among our ancestors; counsel for defendant arguing that this particular statute came within its rule that statutes against law and reason are void. And, again, another relic of past beliefs, which has also been referred to, came out when the Court, in its rather extravagant laudation of international law, expressed the opinion that the *primary* law of nations is but the *law of nature,* and that no state can prejudice or alter any part of such law. But it was admitted that this did not extend to those portions of international law which prevail merely by *tacit consent.*

Much was written, too, of the question whether the occupation of plaintiff's premises had or had not been for military purposes; and the opinion was clear that any occupation for other purposes would not relieve the defendant. The license of the Commissary General was held to be mere usurpation, for such authority belonged, under international law, only to the Commander-in-Chief, and "the rights of the British Gen-

---

[7] The opinion (pp. 39-41) shows that counsel had put instances which the broad language of the Act included, but which were plainly not meant to be within the Act. The case of American prisoners of war incarcerated by the British in houses in New York is mentioned by the Court as one of these, and the question asked whether they are liable to the owners for rent, but the illustration,—though a good enough one of an instance in which a Court cannot follow absolutely the literal words of a statute,—has no real bearing on the main question.

eral . . . could only be communicated by his immediate authority."

The decision finally arrived at was a half-way one, and held the defendant liable for the period during which he had held under the Commissary General, but not liable for his term directly under the Commander-in-Chief. International law, it was said, recognized the right of the latter to use the premises and to lease them, and the Court would presume that the Legislature did not mean to violate this principle, which (so the Court said) could be violated by no nation, and far less by any one of our States, whose powers as to external matters were vested in Congress.

Rutgers v. Waddington cannot, therefore, be classed among the decisions of the period, which claim a right for the Judiciary to inquire into the constitutionality of laws. The language of the opinion expressly renounced any such claim; and it does not seem possible to formulate in words what was the effect of the *judgment,* in the technical sense of lawyers and the law. But the ultimate technical sense of a judicial ruling is not always that which has the greatest influence, and the most palpable point about this case was that, precisely as in cases where the right of the Judiciary was broadly claimed, a plain and positive statute was largely set aside by the Court, and a very different rule of law applied. This was, of course, the feature which appealed to the multitude, unlearned in the law. Their statute was blotted out of existence.

Nor was it only the uneducated to whom this result was the striking fact in the case. The public in general so regarded the matter, and the decision excited great interest among large numbers of people. On September 13, a mass-meeting was called in New York to consider the subject, and a committee appointed to draw up an "Address to the People of the State." This committee, of which Melancthon Smith was one, published a long address,[8] summing up the procedure and then going on to say:

From this state of the case it appears that the Mayor's Court have assumed and exercised a power to set aside an Act of the State. . . . That there should be a power vested in the Courts of Judicature, whereby they might control the supreme Legislative power we think is absurd in itself.

Nor did the matter go unnoticed at the meeting of the Legislature in October, but resolutions were passed, by 25 to 15, that the decision was subversive of all law and good order, because

If a Court . . . may take upon them to dispense with and act in direct violation of a plain and known law of the State, all other Courts, whether superior or inferior, may do the like; and therewith will end all our dear-bought rights and privileges, and Legislatures become useless.

Another resolution, calling for the appointment of a Mayor and Recorder who should govern themselves by the known laws of the land, was defeated by 9 votes to 31.

[8] Reproduced in Dawson's pamphlet from *The New York Packet and the American Advertiser* of November 4, 1784.

It may, in conclusion, be safely said of Rutgers *v.* Waddington that, in spite of the fact that the Court by no means claimed the power since possessed by our American courts, its action came at least very close, as a matter of fact, to assuming and exercising such power, and the public in general so regarded the case. It was thus highly educative, and so constitutes a milestone in the general history of the matter.

The specific point actually presented on the record was the question: What was to be done when the rights involved in a law-suit were found to depend on the provisions of a State statute, which were in conflict with some authorized action of the Central Government? This was at that time a vital question to America, on account of the serious disputes with Great Britain in regard to the Treaty, and its consideration was by no means confined to the Courts.

Congress considered in several instances the subject of violations of the Treaty of Peace. On May 30, 1783, Hamilton reported[9] from a committee consisting of himself, Ellsworth, Izard, Madison, and Hawkins, which had been appointed to inquire what further steps were proper to be taken for carrying into effect the stipulations of the Treaty of Peace. The resolutions which they proposed recited the 4th, 5th, and 6th clauses of the Treaty[10] and the desire to give them speedy effect; and then went on that the several States "be required, and they are hereby required to remove

[9] "Journals of Congress," ed. of 1823, Vol. IV, pp. 224, 225.
[10] These provided respectively that creditors should meet with no lawful impediment to "the recovery of the full value of all *bona fide* debts"; that Congress should earnestly recommend to

all obstructions which may interpose in the way of the entire and faithful execution of the 4th and 6th articles," and again earnestly recommend them to take into serious consideration the 5th article and to conform to it in a spirit of moderation. The resolutions were, however, committed, and do not seem to have come up again.

But when, on January 14, 1784, the definitive Treaty was ratified and proclaimed, a resolution was passed in conformity with a clause of the treaty, recommending to the Legislatures of the States to provide for the restitution of confiscated property, and that they should revise their laws in the premises, so as to conform to justice and equity.[11] This resolution was sent to all the States; and on May 3, 1786, in pursuance of the directions of Congress, the Secretary for Foreign Affairs wrote a circular letter to the Governors, inquiring in regard to their compliance therewith.[12] Here, we must leave the halls of Congress for the moment, in order to inquire what had been done meanwhile in the States.

Their action in the matter is most striking; for in several the Courts had held that State laws, which violated the Treaty, were of no validity, because of such violation, and had declined to enforce them. These rulings have largely fallen into oblivion, and they were

the States the restitution of confiscated property, and the revision of all laws regarding the same; and that no future confiscation should be made nor any prosecution begun against any one because of the part taken by him in the war.

[11] *Ibid.*, pp. 323-327.
[12] "American State Papers, Foreign Relations," Vol. I, p. 228, appendix No. 31.

probably never widely known; but their existence seems to be beyond doubt. In his long letter[13] of May 29, 1792, to the British minister, defending our general course, Jefferson wrote that "treaties made by Congress according to the Confederation were superior to the laws of the States," and then went on to detail instances in which this had been held. In Rhode Island, he wrote:[14]

The attorney for the U. S. in that state, speaking of an act passed before the treaty, says, "This act was considered by our courts as *annulled by the treaty of peace*,[15] and subsequent to the ratification thereof, no proceedings have been had thereon."

The Governor of Connecticut, he added, wrote that

the VIth article of the treaty was immediately observed on receiving the same with the proclamation of Con-

[13] Jefferson's "Writings" by Paul Leicester Ford, Vol. VI, pp. 7 *et seq.*, or "American State Papers (Foreign Relations)," Vol. I, pp. 201 *et seq.* Mr. Ford has printed an early draft of the letter, with comments made by some to whom it was submitted; while the State Papers contain the letter as sent, with many appendices which are useful to us here. My account and quotations are from the Writings, except where I have noted otherwise. Jefferson's view as to the superiority of treaties to the laws of the States was not devised in order to make out his case and deceive the British minister. He had written John Adams from Paris on Feb. 23, 1787: "It has accordingly been the decision of our courts, that the confederation is a part of the law of the land, and superior in authority to the ordinary laws, because it cannot be altered by the legislature of any one state," John Adams's "Life and Works," Vol. IV, pp. 579, 580.

[14] "Writings," Vol. VI, p. 43, or "State Papers," Vol. I, Appendix No. 19, pp. 224, 225.

[15] Italics in original.

gress; the Courts of justice adopted it as a *principle of law*.[15] No further prosecutions were instituted against any person who came within that article, & all such prosecutions as were then pending were discontinued.[16]

In Pennsylvania, Jefferson went on, the Attorney for the United States said that

the Judges have uniformly, and without hesitation, declared in favor of the treaty, on account of it's [sic] being the supreme law of the land. On this ground, they have not only discharged attainted traitors from arrest, but have frequently declared that they were entitled by the treaty to protection.[17]

The attorney in New York wrote, so Jefferson summed up that official's report, that

the act of 1782 of that state relative to the debts due to persons within the enemy's lines was, immediately after the treaty, restrained *by the Superior courts of the state*,[15] from operating on British creditors, and that he did not know a single instance to the contrary.[18]

Even Rutgers *v.* Waddington, of which complaint had been made, was, Jefferson added, "a proof that the courts consider the treaty as paramount to the laws of the states."

In Maryland, though a law had earlier compelled

[16] "Writings," Vol. VI, p. 43, or "State Papers," Vol. I, Appendix No. 18, p. 224.
[17] "Writings," Vol. VI, p. 43. And see Respublica *v.* Gordon, 1 Dallas, p. 233.
[18] "Writings," Vol. VI, p. 44.

those owing debts to British subjects to pay them to the State,

yet the judges of the *State* General Court decided that the treaty not only repealed the law for the future, but for the past also, and decreed that the defendant should pay the money again to that British creditor.

And in Virginia, so Jefferson was told by men of eminence,

both court and counsel there avowed the opinion that the treaty would control any law of the State opposed to it.[19]

It must next be shown what further was done in the matter by Congress. The resolution of January 14, 1784, calling upon the States to revise their laws

[19] *Ibid.* Massachusetts had also reached much the same conclusion (Jefferson's letter to Hammond, *ut supra*, p. 62), and her ruling in this matter seems to be the instance referred to in the letter,—well known to students of this subject,—of J. B. Cutting to Jefferson, dated July 11, 1788 (Bancroft's "Constitution of the United States," Vol. II, p. 472, or "Proceedings of the Mass. Histor. Society," 2d series, Vol. XVII, p. 507). This decision, as stated by Cutting, seemed to be on all fours with Holmes *v.* Walton and Trevett *v.* Weeden, but A. C. Goodell, Jr., editor of the "Acts and Resolves of the Province of Massachusetts Bay," identified it (*Harvard Law Review,* Vol. VII, pp. 415-424) as probably one in which the State Courts held void certain "Resolves" of their Legislature denying interest during the war to British creditors, as being in conflict with the Treaty of Peace. This view of Mr. Goodell is further strengthened by Jefferson's letter to Hammond (*ubi supra*), where he writes of Massachusetts' course as to the vexed question of interest during the war, and says that her courts changed their ruling upon the subject, and in the end held that such interest was recoverable,—much as the cases found by Mr. Goodell seem to show.

so as to make them conform to the Treaty, and the letter of May 3, 1786, from the Secretary for Foreign Affairs to each State, asking what had been done in compliance therewith, have been mentioned. However, before many answers came in to this inquiry Congress took another step in the matter, which is most indicative in regard to the subject-matter of this book. They recommended that all the States should adopt very closely the method, which (as has just been shown) some of the State Judiciaries had adopted *ex mero motu suo,* and that all should pass a statute in the same words,[20] directing their courts to hold void any law of their particular State found to be in conflict with the Treaty.

This resort to the Judicial Department in such a matter would have been in the highest degree unlikely in any people who had not our history back of them, but to us it was almost second nature, for use had, as the great poet says it will, bred a habit in us. Though nothing, so far as I know, shows affirmatively the influences which guided the members of Congress in their action, yet it can hardly be doubted that the recent decisions of the Courts in some of the States, which have been mentioned, were the immediate exciting causes, while back of this lay the beliefs and

---

[20] Called by Brinton Coxe ("Judicial Power," etc., pp. 274, 275, *et seq*). "The Identical Law," under which name I shall refer to it in later pages. It was a sort of predecessor of the "uniform laws" of modern days. All the States except New Hampshire were probably represented on this vote. Varnum, of Trevett *v.* Weeden fame, represented Rhode Island. Frank E. Melvin's "The Judicial Bulwark of the Constitution" in *The Amer. Polit. Science Review,* Vol. VIII, p. 173.

the occasional actions of our people almost since their foundation.

Congress unanimously recommended on March 21, 1787, that each State should enact a law in the following words:

Whereas certain laws made and passed in some of the United States are regarded and complained of as repugnant to the treaty of peace with Great Britain . . . And whereas justice to Great Britain, as well as regard to the honor and interest of the United States, require that the said treaty be faithfully executed, and that all obstacles thereto, and particularly such as do or may be construed to proceed from the laws of this state, be effectually removed.

Therefore be it enacted by [whatever the State's name be] and it is hereby enacted by the authority of the same, that such of the acts or parts of acts of the legislature of this state, as are repugnant to the treaty of peace . . . hereby are repealed. And further that the courts of law and equity within this state be and they hereby are directed and required in all causes and questions cognizable by them respectively, and arising from or touching the said treaty, to decide and adjudge according to the tenor, true intent and meaning of the same, anything in the said acts, or parts of acts, to the contrary thereof in any wise notwithstanding.[21]

A few days later (April 13) Congress sent this recommendation to all the States, with a circular letter, which evidences even more plainly their belief as to the

[21] *Journals of Congress*, edition of 1823, Vol. IV, p. 730.

function of the Judiciary in the matter of unconstitutional laws. It read in part:

Such a general law, would, we think, be preferable to one that should minutely enumerate the acts and clauses intended to be repealed: because omissions might accidentally be made in the enumeration, or questions might arise, and perhaps not be satisfactorily determined, respecting particular laws or clauses, about which contrary opinions may be entertained. By repealing in general terms all acts and clauses repugnant to the treaty, *the business will be turned over to its proper department, viz., the judicial;*[22] and the courts of law will find no difficulty in deciding whether any particular act or clause is or is not contrary to the treaty.[23]

This recommendation found some response from the States, and the proposed law was in its main features adopted by Massachusetts, Rhode Island, Connecticut, New York, Delaware, Maryland, and North Carolina. New Jersey and Pennsylvania declared that no law existed with them contrary to the Treaty with Great Britain.[24]

---

[22] Italics mine.
[23] *Journals of Congress*, edition of 1823, Vol. IV, pp. 735-738.
[24] Jefferson's "Writings" by Ford, Vol. VI, p. 42, or "American State Papers, Foreign Relations," Vol. I, pp. 228-231, Appendices Nos. 32-41 and 43. New Hampshire (*ibid.* Appendix No. 32) had already, apparently in response to the resolution of Congress of January 14, 1784, repealed generally all laws of hers repugnant to the Treaty, but had not specifically referred the matter to the Judiciary. Massachusetts, Connecticut, New York, and Delaware enacted the proposed law almost *verbatim*, while Maryland and North Carolina respectively declared the Treaty to be "the supreme law within this State," or "a part of the

Six or (if Rhode Island is to be included) seven States, therefore, had direct recourse to the Judicial Department to decide what laws stood upon their statute-books in violation of the Treaty of Peace. The Courts were to compare the laws of the State with the more fundamental Treaty and, if they found the State law in conflict with it, were to enter a decree as if the State law had not been in existence. In other words, they were to hold that the latter was unauthorized, that the Legislature had not the power to pass it. Such recourse to the courts was most natural to us with our history, and it is hardly possible to doubt that the conferring and exercise of this function greatly tended to establish and confirm the growing belief in the right of the courts to hold laws unconstitutional.

law of the land," and directed their courts to follow it. Rhode Island declared it a law of the land, "fully binding upon all the citizens of this State," but did not otherwise call upon the Judicial Department.

CHAPTER VI

REVIEW. BAYARD *v.* SINGLETON

AN effort has been made in the preceding pages to trace out certain public beliefs held among our colonial ancestors during the century and a half or so that preceeded the beginnings of independence, in so far as they seem to have a bearing upon the subject of this book. The record is, at best, very incomplete, and has as yet been but little investigated by students in the slow turning over of the pages of our colonial history; but some indications of importance have been found by them, and I think that unprejudiced observers will agree that those days have been shown to have led directly and most naturally to the beliefs and governmental principles of our later years.

Before going on to the work of the Federal Convention, it will be well to try and gather together in a few words the influences of these earlier days, which tended to lead our ancestors towards that Power of the Judiciary, with which this book is concerned and into which it has been shown that they were rapidly drifting before May, 1787.

There are undoubtedly some hints, but no positive proof, that colonial courts occasionally exercised that very power of finding that a statute of their Legislature was unauthorized by its powers, and hence of declining to carry it into effect, with which we are concerned.   One such instance seems even to be pretty clearly shown from the English records, and one colonial judge, beyond doubt, had the matter in mind, and queried what a court ought to do when a pending case turned on an unauthorized colonial enactment. These indications are, however, far too slight to carry conviction, and they cannot possibly be followed up now and the truth be discovered from the vast mass of records under which it lies deeply buried.

Other indications are of far greater importance. There is demonstration that the courts, and men in public life generally, were full of the idea of fundamental principles of justice, which could not be transgressed by the legislative or any authority, and which it was the special function of the courts to exercise and to maintain against the Legislature and all other agencies.   As a modern author wrote: "The law of God, the law of nature, was looked upon as the true law" by the colonists, and all temporal legislation considered binding only as it was an expression of this.   Or, as a writer of the earlier day has been seen to have put it, man has the power *"jus dicere* only; *jus dare,* strictly speaking, belongs alone to GOD."[1]

[1] Paul Samuel Reinsch in "The English Common Law in the Early American Colonies: Select Essays in Anglo-American Legal History," Vol. I, p. 413. Justice Gray wrote of Coke's similar doctrine that it "was repeatedly asserted by Otis and was a favorite in the colonies before the Revolution." Article on "Writs of Assistance," printed in Quincy's (Mass.) Reports, Appendix I, pp. 395-540: see especially pp. 527, 528. See *ante,* p. 34.

Coke's doctrine in Bonham's case was, too, a leading element and, in general nature, very similar to that of fundamental principles; and the reader has seen how it came to the surface in time, soon finding very concrete expression in Stamp Act days and during the early Revolutionary mutterings, when our public men were seeking for a ground on which to justify the action they had decided upon.

Again, every one of the colonies was used to having its statutes, though clothed with all the forms of law, set aside now and then by a higher power as unauthorized by their charter or other organic law, and thus coming to be void. They had many a time seen apparent laws which they had long struggled to secure, and had at last written on their statute-book, come to this untimely end, on the very ground of their being either illegal or not in accordance with a more fundamental law. They struggled in some instances to save these pets of theirs, by reënacting them, or occasionally by some indirect device such as the weak will resort to in a struggle with the strong. They talked of this function, too, knew it well, and at times the opponents of a measure warned its advocates that the proposed law would be thus held unauthorized. The very word *unconstitutional,* with which we are so familiar, was even used, at least in the English records, in this connection.

It is remarkable how closely the action of the Privy Council, in a few of these cases, resembled the action of our American courts in modern days in holding a statute unconstitutional, and hence refusing to carry it out. Thus, Rhode Island passed a law, about 1703, to create an admiralty court. The law was objected to, and Attorney-General Northey, to whom it was referred for his opinion, reported that the charter of Rhode Island gave no power to create an admiralty court. Thereupon, though the charter did not at all provide for a royal veto, the law was recommended for disallowance, and then promptly disallowed by the King in Council.[2] The ground of the conclusion evidently was that the law was not authorized by the charter, was *ultra vires*,—as we say to-day of a corporation's like acts,—or unconstitutional, as we say of statutes not authorized by the fundamental law.

Very much the same result was reached, too, by strictly judicial methods, which far more nearly resemble the function of the courts with which we are so familiar. It seems that now and then, even in ordinary law-suits in Westminster Hall,[3] when the decision depended upon some colonial statute, the Courts held the statute unauthorized, and refused to enforce it on this ground. But far more frequent were the instances of direct appeals to the Privy Council from a decree of a colonial court. Both these classes were quite different technically from the disallowance of laws by the King in Council, but the result both in cases of disallowance and in those of judicial appeals was too much alike for any but the scientific student to hold the distinction

[2] Dickerson's "American Colonial Government," p. 235.
[3] I think such cases are well known to have occurred, but am not aware of any direct proof of the matter, except what is contained in the opinions of Yorke and Talbot in 1732, and of Pratt and Yorke in 1750, quoted *ante*, pp. 42, 43.

clearly before him. The two classes together num-
bered several hundreds; and it is as plain as the noon-
day sun that the voiding of laws passed by the colonial
legislatures was a very vital matter to the colonists.
So well known was it, even to the mass of the people,
that the King's action in the matter was extensively
used in 1776 as a means of appeal to the popular heart,
by those who guided movements and wrote the Declaration of Independence.

Here was a considerable body of legislative and
of judicial action, as well as of theoretical belief,
during colonial times, which could not but tend to
throw doubt upon the applicability to our Legislatures'
actions of the British doctrine of the omnipotence of
Parliament. Nor must it be forgotten that this British
doctrine was one which the colonists thoroughly de-
tested. They had had their experience of omnipotence
and wanted no more of it. A people with this feeling
ground into them, and accustomed for about a century
and a half to see the statutes of its legislative authority set aside in a number of instances as unauthorized,
and the citizens of which often had a hand in leading
up to this result,—even discussing whether some
proposed law lay within the competence of their law-
making body or not,—was ripe for the acceptance of
the belief that their Legislature was strictly limited
and for the discovery of some agency within their
own limits which should exercise this function of controlling the Legislature, when once the connection with
the British Empire should be severed.

Nor, as a matter of fact, did many years pass by

after 1776, before the agency in question was found in the Courts. The circumstances almost inevitably forced the duty upon them; for cases were soon presented in which the right of one of the parties to a litigation depended upon some statute of the Legislature passed in direct defiance of plain provisions of the fundamental law or Constitution, while the other party asserted the provisions of the Constitution as his shield and protection, and called aloud for their maintenance. On the one side was a statute passed by an ephemeral Legislature, on the other side a provision of that fundamental Constitution, to which the Court and the Legislature both owed their very existence, but which the latter had undertaken to violate. If the new device of written Constitutions meant anything,—unless the provisions of these instruments were at once to be allowed to drop into inanity as mere unenforceable words,—how could the court do otherwise than follow the fundamental law and refuse to carry into effect the wrongful, unauthorized, or even directly forbidden, statute?

They, at least, did quickly follow this course, and in a number of instances, scattered throughout our newborn country, the Judiciary refused to carry into effect laws of their Legislature passed in violation of their Constitution. They made then no sweeping claim of authority, specially vested in them, to interpret the Constitution finally and conclusively for all the great agencies of government or for all the world. Their claim was much more modest, and merely went to the effect that when they, one of the great agencies, or

Departments of Government, were officially called upon to act under a statute, which was asserted by one of the parties to the suit to be in violation of the Constitution, the Court must examine this question for itself independently, and that *its own action* must be in accordance with the conclusion at which it arrived.

Prior pages have shown the instances in which the State Courts thus held State laws void, for the reason that they violated some provision of the Constitution of the State. And it has also been shown that cases arose in many different parts of the country, where a State law violated the Treaty of Peace or some other authorized action of Congress, and was for this reason held void. These latter were cases which called imperatively for some cure, or foreign interference by war might well have ruined us, and Congress and our public men sought persistently for the best way out of the trouble. It has been seen that finally,—so far had by that time grown the belief in the function of the Judiciary to prevent the enforcement of unconstitutional laws,—Congress recommended the adoption by all the States of an "Identical Law," expressly drafted for the purpose of referring all such questions of State laws violating the Treaty of Peace to the Judiciary in each State for decision in ordinary law-suits.

It would not be easy to imagine a course of action that would show more clearly than this does the widespread belief in the power of the Judiciary, which is the subject of this book, and to all the evidence that has already been summed up is to be added the assertion or recognition of the power in a number of instances by courts, in proceedings where the question was not technically presented, as well as by other governmental agencies, and even in the private discussions of individuals of note.

Nor was there any let-up in the gathering evidence of our American Doctrine. During the very sittings of the Constitutional Convention of 1787, to which we shall soon turn, still another case directly in point was adjudged in North Carolina, again asserting most clearly the Power of the Judiciary in regard to unconstitutional laws. But Bayard v. Singleton [4] is not only instructive from the opinion and the technical judgment. It had also back of it a history of several years, in which the subject was at times very actively debated, and leading men wrote letters so plain that he who runs may read; their design being to convince the public in North Carolina of the Judicial Power, and to lead to a decision denying effect to certain laws of the State.

During the Revolution many of our States took proceedings to confiscate the property of the Tories, and the struggle in this matter lasted for a number of years after the Peace. North Carolina was one such State, and several violent and inexcusable laws having this object in view were put upon her statute-books. Apparently the forfeitures were made under general laws, and there was later appointed a Board of Commissioners of Forfeited Estates, whose duty it was to sell the lands, the proceeds to go into the coffers of the State. Troubles seem to have cropped up in the enforcement

[4] 1 Martin, p. 42.

of this system, and, at least after the war was over, there was a great deal of opposition among leading men to the violent laws that were passed by the Legislature in the effort to carry through the system upon which they had entered.

At the session of 1785, one such law of a very ultra character was passed, which was euphemistically called, "The Quieting and Confirming Act."[5] It seems that people had not always submitted with due docility to the conclusions as to forfeitures reached by the Commissioners, but had sought protection in the Courts after the sale of their lands by this Board; so the Quieting Act was passed, under the provisions of which, whenever in an ejectment-suit the defendant should file an affidavit that he had bought from the Commissioners the suit should be at once, without more, dismissed. No inquiry was to be allowed whether or not the former owner ever had been a Tory, nor even whether he had been the actual owner of the lands. All was to be left, as had been decided during the passion and hatred of a civil war, under the inspiration, perhaps of jealousy, or envy, and upon no better evidence than that of the merest slander dropped by many-tongued Rumor.

Of course, opposition to such a law cropped up

[5] "Public Acts of the General Assembly of North Carolina, for 1785," Chapter 7 (Newbern, 1804), Vol. I, p. 396. The session began November 19, 1785, but the date of the law is not given. The provisions of the statute were modified at the session of 1786 by a statute which recited that doubts had arisen in regard to the act of 1785, and authorized suits to be brought by citizens, provided they did not hold title from any one named in the Confiscation Acts (*Ibid.,* Cap. 6, 1786, p. 414).

quickly, and it became the center of a long and hard contest. James Iredell,—who had been appointed a Judge of the Superior Court of North Carolina in 1777, but who resigned the next year, and was in 1789 appointed to the Supreme Court of the United States, which position he held with honor and credit until his death in 1799,—was a leader in this contest. He had sided with the colonies during the Revolution, but was an Englishman by birth; and doubtless here was one cause which led him to oppose an Act sure to bring great hardship and the gravest injustice to some of his friends and relatives. A correspondent wrote to Iredell, on January 19, 1786, of

the wonderful law by which the Assembly have arrogated to themselves the judicial power in all suits regarding confiscation. How the people at large will like the innovation I know not.[6]

And but ten days later Iredell wrote to another correspondent:

No consideration under Heaven shall induce me, directly or indirectly, to support, countenance or have *act* or *part* in carrying so infamous a law into execution.[7]

We shall see that he adhered firmly to this resolution.

Still another correspondent wrote to Iredell about a month later, denouncing the law in good, set terms,

[6] "The Life and Correspondence of James Iredell," by G. J. McRee, Vol. II, p. 132.
[7] *Ibid.*, p. 133.

and perhaps opening the door of truth in his references to their being at the mercy of a set of "greedy and rapacious Commissioners," and then went on to urge Iredell to action.

I wish that you could do something more than give advice, as I am persuaded that if the Judges are beset by the principal gentlemen of the bar in a proper manner, they will not venture to go any great lengths.[8]

Perhaps it was more or less in consequence of this request that Iredell wrote and published in a New-bern paper of August 17, 1786, his well-known letter upon the subject in general, over the signature "Elector," addressed "To the Public."[9] It is a very remarkable paper and shows that its writer saw the whole subject very clearly. From whatever source his knowledge came, Iredell understood the nature and the necessity of the matter as plainly as it can be shown, so far as I know, that any of his countrymen then did.

The letter referred to the anxiety felt at the time their State Constitution was formed, and goes on to say that

It was of course to be considered how to impose restrictions on the legislature, that might still leave it free to all useful purposes, but at the same time guard against the abuse of unlimited power. We were all, he went on in substance, disgusted with the British language of the

[8] *Ibid.*, pp. 137, 138.
[9] *Ibid.*, pp. 145-149. This letter is reproduced in Coxe's "Judicial Power," etc., pp. 253-258.

omnipotence of Parliament, and we felt its mischiefs. "I have therefore no doubt but that the power of the Assembly is limited and defined by the constitution. It is a *creature* of the constitution. . . . The great argument is, that though the Assembly have not a *right* to violate the constitution, yet if they *in fact* do so, the only remedy is, either by a humble petition that the law may be repealed, or a universal resistance of the people. . . . [After arguing the insufficiency of these two remedies]. These two remedies then being rejected, it remains to be inquired whether the judicial power hath any authority to interfere in such a case. The duty of that power, I conceive, in all cases, is to decide according to the *laws of the State.* It will not be denied, I suppose, that the Constitution is a *law of the State,* as well as an act of Assembly, with this difference only that it is the *fundamental* law, and unalterable by the Legislature, which derives all its power from it. One act of Assembly may repeal another act of Assembly. For this reason, the latter is to be obeyed, and not the former. An act of Assembly cannot repeal the constitution, or any part of it. For that reason, an act of Assembly, inconsistent with the constitution, is *void,* and cannot be obeyed, without disobeying the superior law to which we were previously and irrevocably bound. The judges, therefore, must take care at their peril, that every act of Assembly they presume to enforce is warranted by the constitution, since if it is not, they act without lawful authority. This is not a usurped or a discretionary power, but one inevitably resulting from the constitution of their office, they being judges *for the benefit of the whole people,* not *mere servants of the Assembly.*

The Elector went on to say that the county courts have the like power, and that

the objection . . . urged by some persons, that sheriffs and other ministerial officers must do the same, does not apply, for the power of judging rests with the courts, and their decision is final. Did a sheriff ever refuse to hang a man because he thought him unjustly convicted?

Beyond all doubt, one chief purpose of this letter was to influence the Supreme Court of North Carolina, before which a case had come up at Newbern three months earlier (May, 1786), wherein the constitutionality of the Quieting and Confirming Act had been argued, but which case the court had not decided. The judges had evidently looked upon the question as too serious and too difficult to be disposed of offhand, and had held it open for consideration. The case referred to was, of course, Bayard *v.* Singleton. It was an ejectment brought by the prior owner,—whose land had been forfeited under the Sate laws,—against the defendant, who held under a title derived from a sale and purchase from the Commissioners of Forfeited Estates. The plaintiff was represented at different times,—perhaps all through the litigation,—by James Iredell, Samuel Johnson, and William R. Davie, while the defendant's counsel were Abner Nash and Alfred Moore. The case was heard for the first time, probably in the end of May, 1786, and the Judges sitting were Ashe, Spencer, and Williams.[10]

[10] My account of the case at this stage is derived from the official report in 1 Martin, p. 42 *et seq.;* from the *Pennsylvania Packet and Daily Advertiser* of Philadelphia, July 1, 1786, con-

Defendant's counsel, Nash, at once filed the necessary affidavit, setting forth that his client had purchased from the Commissioners of Forfeited Estates, and then moved to dismiss in accordance with the directions of the Quieting Act. This motion, the official report,—which was written by Judge Spencer,—records, "brought on long arguments from the counsel on each side, on constitutional points," but the Court held the case under advisement, the same report goes on, after remarks not to show a "single sentiment" as to the law. These cold and meager details are pieced out by the newspaper accounts, which have it that

The plaintiff's lawyers warmly exclaimed against a law, enacted to punish offenses committed a long time before its taking place; they argued that it being an article of our bill of rights, that *retrospective laws are oppressive, unjust, and incompatible with liberty, wherefore no* ex post facto *law ought to be made,* the Assembly had clearly exceeded the limits of the power which the people in whom all political power is vested, and from whom, solely, it derives, had delegated to their representatives met in general assembly, and that an act so illegally passed, was not to be looked on as a law. . . .

Col. Davie, particularly, sustained these arguments with so much warmth and energy, that the grand jury, considering his free investigation of the Assembly's conduct, as a criminal step, in its nature injurious to, and

taining a news item dated "Newbern (N. C.), June 7," and from the same journal of August 23, 1786, containing a Newbern item dated June 1, which speaks of the court's adjournment. *See* also Battle's "Address on the History of the Supreme Court," in 103 North Carolina Reports, pp. 445 *et seq.;* 470, 471; and Coxe's "Judicial Power," etc., pp. 248-267.

destructive of, and against the peace and dignity of the State, presented him on the 27th ult., but the judges, either more indulgent, or better acquainted with the rights of a lawyer defending his client, or an unprejudiced citizen the liberty of his country, discharged him. . . . The defendant's lawyers pleaded that all Acts of Assembly were laws, and their execution could not be prevented. The judges, unwilling to approve of a law which seems unconstitutional, or of disapproving an act of the Legislature without the most mature consideration, have declined giving an immediate decision.

The newspaper of the later date specifies the following as part of the language of Davie in his argument, for which he was "presented,"

that the act of Assembly . . . was in every respect unjust, and expressly against the constitution, that the said act was the arbitrary edict of a leading party or faction of the Assembly; and that although it was passed by the Assembly, the said act was null and void, and not law; and ought not to be obeyed by the people; or words fully to those purposes. That he considered the Assembly and commissioners as one, and that they had violently and unjustly seized the property of the people, with many other assertions, saying "the commissioners were the creatures of the Assembly." The court took no steps in the affair, but it is understood that the Assembly will.

For a year from this time the case remained quiescent, so far as known. It was during the summer following this first hearing that Iredell's letter of an "Elector" was published, and probably many other now forgotten discussions of the case were held in one way or another. Doubtless, as has been already suggested, Iredell's letter was intended to influence the Court, and perhaps it was the cause which led to his being taken into the case. Nothing, so far as I know, shows that he had any hand in the litigation until the second argument in May, 1787, but he seems then to have taken the laboring oar at first held by Davie. In May, 1787, Davie was far off in Philadelphia, a member of the Constitutional Convention.

The second hearing was on May 30,[11] 1787, at Newbern, when the official report tells us that Nash's motion to dismiss was renewed and that there was a "very lengthy debate from the bar." The Court recommended the parties to consent to a fair decision of the property in question by a jury, according to the common law of the land, but this proposal, as well as some other one of a like nature, failed.

The official report continues:

The court then after every reasonable endeavor had been used in vain for avoiding a disagreeable difference between the Legislature and the judicial powers of the

[11] *The Pennsylvania Packet,* etc., of June 23, 1787, contains an item "Newbern, May 31," reading: "Yesterday was agitated the celebrated question—whether the suits brought for the recovery of confiscated property should be dismissed, according to the act of Assembly called the *Quieting Act*—when the Court gave their opinion in the negative." Prof. William S. Carpenter ("Judicial Tenure in the United States," Yale University Press, 1918, p. 19) writes, on the authority of the *Maryland Gazette* of July 3, 1787, that the case was decided on May 29.

state, at length with much apparent reluctance,[12] but with great deliberation and firmness, gave their opinion separately, but unanimously for overruling the aforementioned motion for the dismission of the said suits.

In the course of which the judges observed, that the obligation of their oaths, and the duty of their office required them in that situation, to give their opinion on that important and momentous subject; and that notwithstanding the great reluctance they might feel against involving themselves in a dispute with the Legislature of the state, yet no object of concern or respect could come in competition or authorize them to dispense with the duty they owed the public, in consequence of the trust they were invested with under the solemnity of their oaths. . . .

That by the constitution every citizen had undoubtedly a right to a decision of his property by a trial by jury. For that if the Legislature could take away this right, and require him to stand condemned in his property without a trial, it might with as much authority require his life to be taken away without a trial by jury, and that he should stand condemned to die, without the formality of any trial at all: that if the members of the General Assembly could do this, they might with equal authority, not only render themselves the legislators of the state for life, without any further election by the people, from thence transmit the dignity and authority of legislation down to their heirs male forever. . . .

[12] Iredell wrote Spaight in August of the "infinite reluctance [with which] the judges came to this decision, [and] what pains they took by proposing expedients to obviate its necessity"; see *infra,* p. 121.

It is interesting, too, to see that, as Brinton Coxe pointed out,[13] the Court adopted the argument of Varnum one year earlier in Trevett v. Weeden and dating back to Vattel that, by passing an act to alter the Constitution, the Legislature would at once destroy its own existence as a Legislature and dissolve the government established by the Constitution.

Nash's motion to dismiss was refused, and there was a trial, the report goes on, at which the main question was in regard to the right of an alien to hold land in North Carolina. Upon the decision of this case, so the report concludes,

twenty-seven others depending in the same court upon similar, or less substantial grounds, were all swept off the docket, by non-suits voluntarily suffered.

The triumph was a great one, and it shows very clearly how far and how wide the principle lying at the base of the decision had by this time spread. Judges and counsel were none the less bold men thus to tear down a system, doubtless wrongful and unjust, but having back of it a strong popular support, as well as the overwhelming voice of the legislative body. To Iredell is certainly due much of the credit; while Davie, the leader at the first hearing, and who had been threatened with criminal process for his outspoken denunciation of the law as null and void, was, at the time of the second hearing, sitting in the Constitutional Convention at Philadelphia, and cannot pos-

[13] "Judicial Power," etc., p. 251. For Varnum's argument in Trevett v. Weeden, see *ante*, p. 70.

sibly have forgotten his former argument nor have failed to hear of the final result of the case, when the Convention still had a mass of work ahead of it. The decision in Bayard *v.* Singleton and the other earlier cases pointed clearly enough to a mode of solving some of their immensely difficult problems.

It has been said that some writers hold the view that the early decisions refusing to execute an unconstitutional law remained known to but few, and thus had little influence. This has already been clearly shown to be a grave error as to some of them, notably Trevett *v.* Weeden and Rutgers *v.* Waddington, while the striking similarity of the arguments advanced by counsel has also just been seen. Bayard *v.* Singleton, too, had much of North Carolina by the ears from the early days of the policy in the Legislature, out of which it grew, down to the end, when twenty-seven similar suits fell with it. Wrangled about in the Legislature, discussed in the public papers near and far,—with the eminent General Davie threatened with criminal process for his argument, with many hundred acres of land doubtless snatched back from the purchasers at public sales,—it is impossible to suppose that the decision in this particular case remained hidden under a bushel. Later pages will show, too, how strangely opportune it was for the Convention, and that it seemed to come in the nick of time, when the absolute veto on all State laws was exciting the gravest discontent, and the method of judicial control was looming up in its place.

Of course, by no means all looked upon Bayard *v.* Singleton as did Iredell and Davie. Richard Dobbs Spaight was a colleague of Davie's in the Convention from North Carolina, and utterly disapproved of the decision. On August 12, 1787, he wrote[14] to Iredell from Philadelphia, telling of the recent reference to the Committee of Detail of the resolutions which had resulted from the struggles of the Convention, and then adding:

The late decision of our judges at Newbern must, in my opinion, produce the most serious reflections in the breast of every thinking man and of every well-wisher of his country. [After admitting the injustice of some of the laws passed and declining to defend them, he goes on that it is the judges' usurpation of authority that he complains of. I can find nothing in the Constitution to support them, and it would have been absurd and contrary to the practice of the world, to grant them powers that would have operated as a negative on the proceedings of the Legislature]. The State . . . would be subject to the will of three individuals, who united in their own persons the legislative and judiciary powers, which no monarch in Europe enjoys, and which would be more despotic than the Roman Decemvirate,[15] and equally as insufferable. If they possessed the power, what check or control would there be to their proceedings?

[14] McRee's "Life," etc., of Iredell, Vol. II, pp. 168-171, or Coxe's "Judicial Power," etc., Appendix No. 6, pp. 385, 386.
[15] Evidently this word should be "Triumvirate," as it is written by Battle in his "History of the Supreme Court," 103 N. Ca., pp. 472-473.

Iredell in reply wrote to Spaight, August 26 :[16]

In regard to the late decision at Newbern, I confess it has ever been my opinion, that an act inconsistent with the Constitution was void; and that the judges, consistently with their duties, could not carry it into effect. The Constitution appears to me to be a fundamental law, limiting the powers of the Legislature, and with which every exercise of those powers must, necessarily, be compared. [He next refers to the British Parliament and its absolute power, so that any act passed by it], not *inconsistent with natural justice* (for that curb is avowed by the judges even in England), would have been binding on the people. It really appears to me, the exercise of the power is unavoidable, the Constitution not being a mere imaginary thing. . . . It really seems to me the danger is the most chimerical that can be supposed of this power being abused; and if you had seen as I did, with what infinite reluctance the judges came to this decision, what pains they took by proposing expedients to avoid its necessity, you would have seen in a strong light how little probable it is a judge would ever give such a judgment, where he thought he could possibly avoid it. . . . I believe many think as you do upon this subject, though I have not heard much said about it, and I only speak of the general question, independent of an application to any case whatever. Most of the lawyers, I believe, are of my opinion in regard to that.

By the time of the meeting of the Federal Convention of 1787, therefore, three positive and strictly technical decisions had been rendered, asserting the Courts'

[16] McRee's "Iredell," Vol. II, pp. 172-176, or Coxe's "Judicial Power," pp. 259-263.

power to hold a State law void, because of not being authorized under the State Constitution in as many States (New Jersey, Connecticut, and Rhode Island); and in New York the decision of the Court in Rutgers *v.* Waddington, though not its reasoning, came to much the same result, being generally looked upon as setting aside a law that the court thought unauthorized, without much discrimination in regard to the source of the statute and of the more fundamental law. In two other leading States, moreover,—Virginia and Pennsylvania,—the right of the Judiciary had been recognized in the courts, or by other important administrative agencies, and in New Hampshire it had been asserted and, it might perhaps be added, recognized. Thus, without including those cases turning on violations of the Treaty, which depended upon decisions either of the lower courts or decisions which have not been preserved, in six States out of the thirteen, there had been recognition of the doctrine. For a year, too, before the Convention met, Bayard *v.* Singleton had been under discussion in North Carolina, and its final decision in favor of the judicial power was known to the members of the Convention, while their discussions were still in the inchoate stage of mere resolutions. Before the delegates reached their final conclusions, the leaders must have often discussed the case, and have known that North Carolina was the fourth State to have rendered a positive and undeniable decision that the courts had the power, and were in duty bound, to refuse the aid of their arm in the execution of a statute that was, in their opinion, in violation of the fundamental law.

Behind all this, too, lay as a background our history in the matter during colonial and early Revolutionary days.

CHAPTER VII

THE CONSTITUTIONAL CONVENTION OF 1787. ITS ADOPTION OF THE JUDICIAL METHOD OF VOIDING UNCONSTITUTIONAL LAWS

THE Convention of 1787 was composed in great part of statesmen,—men who had been long in service and had been trained in the old school. They did not think that one man was likely by a week's "intensive study" to work out successfully a new system that would change *in toto* some branch of the system of law and custom, which had grown up by the attrition of thousands of minds during a long course of years. When change became desirable, they were perhaps not quick to recognize the need, but they could do so and would then approach the matter with care and examine the existing system and the defects that had arisen, before they ventured to essay the task of creating a new machine intended to work better. They were thus not often called upon quickly to repeal a law just passed, but which was found impossible to administer, nor were they forever engaged in explaining that the language they had used did not mean what its words plainly imported. The Courts did not have to strain every principle of law and all the rules of language, in order to avoid grave injustice and not to land in chaos.

Numbers of the members of the Convention had served in Congress and knew the recent, as well as the past, history of the country. They knew that our public affairs verged on chaos, that such government as we had could not possibly continue, and that we were very likely in one way or another to lose even that independence which had been won after such efforts. But they knew, too, the exceeding difficulty of amending so as to cure, and they did not write out a new Constitution off-hand,—as did many Frenchmen about 1789,—but went on slowly and laboriously to consider, to compare views, to meet the essential necessities of the very difficult situation, and by this lengthy and wearying process, they brought forth an instrument which, whatever may be its fate after the chaos of to-day's war is passed, at least guided with eminent success for about a century and a quarter the growth and prosperity of a people, very young and powerless at its foundation, but since then gone through a lusty youth and now among the most powerful and capable on earth.

Nearly every question that came up before the members of the Convention during the months of their labor presented great difficulties, but few were so infinitely difficult as that of devising a means,—with some chance of adoption,—to control the States and prevent them from forever violating the laws and the powers of the Central Government. Such laws had been passed by the States under the Confederation in hosts of instances, and had been the means (as has been already shown) of getting us into serious difficulties with foreign nations. The Treaty of Peace with Great Britain had been violated by numbers of the States, and the late Mother Country was in high indignation at the failure of Tories to receive the treatment which she had meant to secure for her late supporters in the colonies. Other countries, too, had plenty of like causes of complaint.[1] Members of Congress had of course seen with especial clearness all the difficulties arising from these general causes, and prior pages have touched upon the efforts and the plans devised to cure such evils while the Confederation lasted.

It would not be rash to assume that numbers of members of the coming Convention compared notes and devised plans for solving the problems ahead of them; but I know of no proof of this, except in regard to some of the delegates from Virginia. That leading State had taken an active part in calling the Convention, and its members felt a degree of responsibility, owing to this cause. Madison evidently gave a deal of thought to the matter, and wrote to others outlining some of his ideas, and in these letters one of the very chief points in his mind was the absolute need of a means to control the separate States. He wrote to Jefferson (then in Europe) on March 19, 1787, telling him of the coming Convention and of some of his ideas in regard to it, and giving as his opinion that it would be expedient "to arm the federal head with a negative *in all cases whatsoever* on the local Legislatures."[2]

[1] See *ante,* pp. 80-82.
[2] "Works," by Congress, 1865, Vol. I, pp. 284-286.

Randolph was also thinking of the work of the Convention, and wrote[3] Madison on March 27, suggesting the introduction of some "general propositions" into the body by Virginia. To this letter Madison replied on April 8 with cordial approval,[4] detailing his views at some length, perhaps a little fearful that Randolph might not agree with his "centralizing" views, but, none the less, setting forth the need of a broad control of the States. And, again, to Washington Madison wrote[5] but a few days later (April 16), urging that positive power in all cases which required uniformity must be vested in the general Government, and once more specifying that

Over and above this positive power, a negative in all cases whatever on the Legislative acts of the States, as heretofore exercised by the Kingly prerogative, appears to me to be absolutely necessary, and to be the least possible encroachment on the State jurisdictions.

When the Virginia deputies arrived in Philadelphia they held conferences together and concluded, much as Randolph had suggested to Madison, that, owing to the prominence of Virginia in the general matter, some initiative step might be expected of them.[6] The resolutions offered by Randolph on May 29th were the outgrowth of these meetings. They contained a rough outline of a government, and the 6th and 8th resolutions read in part as follows:

[3] Conway's "Randolph," p. 71.
[4] Elliot's "Debates," Vol. V, pp. 107, 108.
[5] "Works," by Congress, 1865, Vol. I, p. 287.
[6] Farrand, Vol. III, pp. 539-551, or Elliot, Vol. V, pp. 109-122.

6. That the National Legislature ought to be impowered . . . to negative all laws passed by the several States, contravening in the opinion of the National Legislature the articles of Union, and to call forth the force of the Union against any member of the Union failing to fulfill its duty under the articles thereof. . . .

8. That the Executive, and a convenient number of the National Judiciary, ought to compose a council of revision with authority to examine every act of the National Legislature before it shall operate, & every act of a particular Legislature before a Negative thereon shall be final; and that the dissent of the said Council shall amount to a rejection, unless the Act of the National Legislature be again passed, or that of a particular Legislature be again negatived by ———— of the members of each branch.[7]

I do not know of anything to show who had suggested the idea of joining the Judiciary with the Executive as a Council of Revision,[8] but Madison, at least, supported it; and he and a few other members were most insistent, down to a very late day, in pressing the plan in one form or another, in order to secure the immediate setting aside of harmful laws. He was evidently disappointed, too, at the result; and wrote Jefferson on Oct. 24, 1787,[9] referring to the general power of negative which he had wanted, adding:

[7] Farrand, Vol. I, p. 21.
[8] The idea of such a Council was borrowed from New York, Madison said on August 14, Farrand, Vol. II, p. 291. Frank E. Melvin's "The Judicial Bulwark of the Constitution," in *The Amer. Polit. Science Review,* Vol. VIII, p. 167 *et seq.;* see footnote 23 on page 176.
[9] Farrand, Vol. III, pp. 131-136.

It may be said that the Judicial authority under our new system, will keep the States within their proper limits, and supply the place of a negative on their laws. The answer is, that it is more convenient to prevent the passage of a law than to declare it void after it is passed; that this will be particularly the case, when the law aggrieves individuals, who may be unable to support an appeal against a State to the supreme Judiciary.

It will be necessary to follow here to some extent the actions of the Convention in regard to joining the Judiciary with the Executive as a Council of Revision to approve or disapprove of all laws of Congress and of the States; for not only was this idea pressed in one form or another by Madison and other leading men down to near the adjournment, but some strangely unauthorized conclusions have been drawn by certain modern writers from its rejection.

The power contained in the 6th clause of the Virginia Resolutions, for Congress "to negative all laws, passed by the several States, contravening, in the opinion of the national legislature, the articles of union," was agreed to on May 31.[10] But the 8th clause to establish the proposed Council of Revision was a subject of discussion, and the joining of the Judiciary with the Executive in this function was disapproved by 8 States to 2, on motion of Gerry, on June 4.[11] Gerry could not then have known of the very recent decision in Bayard *v.* Singleton, but he certainly knew of other like cases, for he spoke of them, and drew the

[10] *Ibid.,* Vol. I, p. 47.
[11] *Ibid.,* p. 104

distinction between the power they asserted to decide
on the constitutionality of laws, and the idea of making
the judiciary "judges of the policy of public measures." Two days later (June 6), the same Council of
Revision was again discussed under a motion to re-
consider, but was once more lost by 3 votes to 8;[12] and
on June 8 a motion to extend the already granted powers of Congress in regard to negativing laws of the
States, so that they should have power "to negative
all laws which to them shall appear improper," was
also lost.[13]

At this stage there seems to be an illustration of how
strongly the members felt the need of concession and
compromise, and, again, of how very clear was in
the minds of some of them the right of the Judiciary
in regard to unconstitutional laws. On June 10 Randolph made a communication[14] for conciliating the
small States, one part of which was that, though every
negative of a State law should prevent its operation,
"any State may appeal to the national Judiciary against
a negative; and that such negative if adjudged to be
contrary to the power granted by the articles of Union,
shall be void," and further that "any individual con-
ceiving himself injured or oppressed by the partiality
or injustice of a law of any particular State may resort
to the National Judiciary, who may adjudge such laws
to be void, if found contrary to the principles of equity
and justice." It is, I think, too plain for discussion
from these proposals that Randolph had already a

[12] Farrand, Vol. III. p. 140.
[13] Ibid., pp. 162, 163.
[14] Ibid., Vol. III, pp. 55, 56.

pretty clear comprehension of the general idea of judicial control, and we shall find him[15] later writing another provision in his draft of a constitution to provide for the general exercise of the power by the Judicial Department.

The discussion heretofore had been in Committee of the Whole, and the Committee's report was made on June 13 to the Convention proper. It consisted of nineteen resolutions,[16] one of which (the 6th) gave power to the national legislature "to negative all laws passed by the several States contravening in the opinion of the National Legislature the articles of Union, or any treaties subsisting under the authority of the Union." And the 18th resolution contained a provision, which looks like one more then unseen indication of that doctrine of Judicial Power, which was to come later,—that

the Legislative, Executive, and Judiciary powers within the several States ought to be bound by oath to support the Articles of Union.

The plan in general was looked upon by quite a number of members, particularly from the small States, as highly national and as giving all power to a few large States, and the greatest dissatisfaction was felt, so that, as Madison wrote, there was at this time "serious anxiety for the result of the Convention."

The members in opposition had been holding meetings in the evenings to concert a plan to take the place

[15] *Infra.*, pp. 142, 143.
[16] Farrand, Vol. I, pp. 236-237.

of the proposed system, which they thought so exceptionable. According to Luther Martin, Gerry first proposed these meetings; and Gerry, Mason, the delegates from New Jersey and Connecticut, part of that from Delaware, a member from South Carolina, one from Georgia, and Luther Martin attended at the discussions.[17] It was, of course, as their spokesman that Paterson of New Jersey on June 14th told the Convention that it was the wish of several delegates to prepare a plan purely federal, and said they hoped to present it the next day. They did so and, though their plan[18] adhered largely to requisitions, and was soon set aside as a whole by the Convention, yet one clause (the sixth) became later of vital importance, for it contained the gist of the method which was finally adopted to prevent the operation of unconstitutional laws of the States. It avoided the negative by Congress, which was then still contained in the Report of the Committee of the Whole, and adopted what has since been, if it was not at that very day, called the judicial method of voiding such laws.

The judiciaries of the several States were, according this proposal, to be "bound . . . in their decisions" by authorized laws or treaties of the Central Power, "anything in the respective laws of the Individual States to the contrary notwithstanding," and the federal executive might call forth the power of the confederated States to compel obedience.[19] It is highly

[17] Farrand, Vol. III, pp. 281-286.
[18] *Ibid*, Vol. I, pp. 242-245.
[19] The clause as a whole read as follows "6. Resd. that all Acts of the U. States in Congs. made by virtue & in pur-

likely[20] that during the meetings of the evening caucus,
prior to June 15th, the decision in Bayard *v.* Singleton
at Newbern on May 30 was known in Philadelphia;
and, of course, to Gerry and any others who knew
of the prior like decisions in the country, it pointed
most clearly to the method they had best propose, and
enormously emphasized those precedents and their importance as factors in our public affairs.   Whether it
actually led them to the adoption of the clause they
suggested, and which has just been quoted, is of course
conjecture; but it may well be that such was the case.

It is impossible to attribute to the words that *the
judiciaries in the several States shall be bound in their
decisions* by authorized laws and so on, of Congress,
any meaning but that which has become known as the

suance of the powers hereby & by the articles of confederation
vested in them, and all Treaties made & ratified under the
authority   of the U. States shall be the supreme law of the
respective States so far forth as those Acts or Treaties shall
relate to the said States or their Citizens, and that the Judiciary
of the several States shall be bound thereby in their decisions,
anything in the respective laws of the Individual States to the
contrary notwithstanding; and that if any State, or any body
of men in any State shall oppose or prevent ye. carrying into
execution such acts or treaties, the federal Executive shall be
authorized to call forth ye power of the Confederated States,
or so much thereof as may be necessary to enforce and compel
an obedience to such Acts, or an Observance of such Treaties."

[20] *The Pennsylvania Packet* of June 23 notices the decision,
and I know of no earlier publication in regard to it, but private
letters were probably far more rapid, and some of the friends
of Davie were likely to let him know at once of the decision
of a case in which he had been so active. Brinton Coxe
("Judicial Power," etc., p. 266) estimates that water communication between Newbern and Philadelphia might be made then
in seven or eight days, under favorable circumstances. See
ante, pp. 109-121.

American Doctrine of Judicial Power, and Luther Martin wrote[21] in 1788, in a public controversy with Ellsworth, that the very similar proposal which he offered to the Convention on July 17[22] was intended by him to be *in substitution* for the power, which the Convention had at one time adopted, of a negative by Congress on the laws of the States, which he deemed to be wholly inadmissible.

Here is most persuasive evidence that the clause so offered by Martin, as well as the like clause of the New Jersey Plan, was definitely meant as an adoption of the American Doctrine, which prior pages have shown had made such strides in our country by this date, and there is further circumstantial evidence of the meaning of the men who drafted the New Jersey Plan.

The first actual decision asserting the judicial power had been rendered in New Jersey in the case of Holmes *v.* Walton in 1780. It was decided by Brearly, while Chief Justice of the State, and at the same time William Paterson was Attorney General; William Livingston, Governor, and William C. Houston was the next year Clerk of the Court. The Governor was *ex-officio* Chancellor, and there is even direct evidence (if any be needed) that he was conversant with the doc-

[21] Farrand, Vol. III, pp. 271-275.
[22] It is conceivable that Martin referred to the origin of clause 6 of the New Jersey Plan, but there is nothing to show who made the proposal to the caucus held in June, which became clause 6 of the New Jersey Plan presented to the Convention on June 15, while Martin did himself make the like proposal to the Convention on July 17. *Infra,* pp. 137, 138.

trine of Holmes *v.* Walton,[23] and it is at least highly likely that Houston[24] also knew of it. These four men,—Brearly, Livingston, Paterson, and Houston,— were all members of the New Jersey delegation in the Federal Convention, and as such it is clear, from what Martin wrote, that some, probably all, of them attended the evening meetings of the caucus that offered the New Jersey Plan to the Convention on June 15. It is surely impossible to imagine that they failed to bring into the discussion of a caucus aiming to digest a "purely federal" plan that idea of judicial power, which they had seen exemplified in Holmes *v.* Walton, and which is contained in clause 6 of the New Jersey Plan.

Nor is this all. Gerry, who proposed the meetings to Martin, was the first member of the Convention to

[23] President Austin Scott's article on "The New Jersey Precedent," in Vol. IV, *Amer. Historical Review,* or "Rutgers College Publications, No. 8." I am indebted to this article for nearly all the facts relating to Holmes *v.* Walton.
[24] Houston was a member of Congress from 1779 to 1781, when he accepted the clerkship of the Supreme Court. He was therefore in Congress at the time of the decision of Holmes *v.* Walton, among men likely to hear and talk of it. He had been in the army during the war, and Professor of Mathematics at Princeton, but studied law and was admitted to the bar in 1781. He is shown by the pages of Elliot's "Debates" to have been present in the Convention at its opening, and on July 23rd and possibly on the 17th; while a privately printed sketch of him by Thomas Allan Glenn, Norristown, 1903 (to which my attention was kindly called by his great-grandson, William Churchill Houston, Esq., of Philadelphia), says that there is every reason to believe that he was constant in attendance. He did not sign the constitution, for unknown reasons, but did sign the report of the commissioners. Elliot's mention of him on July 23 shows that he was present much later than the presentation of the New Jersey Plan.

refer in debate (June 4) to the judicial power, and nothing can be plainer than his words, while of the others who, according to Martin, attended the meetings, Mason of Virginia, Martin of Maryland, and Sherman[25] of Connecticut, all expressed themselves the same way long before the adjournment (July 17 and 21); furthermore, Ellsworth and Johnson of Connecticut, Reed, Bassett and Dickinson of Delaware, Charles Pinckney of South Carolina, and Few and Baldwin of Georgia,—from both of which latter two States one member of the delegation attended the meetings,—have all been found to have, at least not very much later in their careers, favored the same view.[26] Thus, Gerry, Mason, Martin, Sherman, and three (or perhaps four) of the five members from New Jersey,— at least seven out of the nine who almost certainly attended the conferences,—were then, or in a few days, in favor of the judicial review. With all this on

[25] Other language used by Sherman at about this same period, whatever may have been its exact connection, shows that he had a full understanding of judicial control. Among his papers was found a document, which Prof. Farrand thinks probably presents the ideas of the Connecticut delegation in forming the New Jersey Plan, while others have thought it was offered to the Convention. It proposed to grant Congress certain additional powers and among these the power "to make laws binding on the people of the United States, and on the courts of law, and other magistrates and officers, civil and military, within the several States, in all cases which concern the common interests of the United States": and it also resolved that "the laws of the United States ought, as far as may be consistent with the common interests of the Union, to be carried into execution by the judiciary and executive officers of the respective States, wherein the execution thereof is required." Farrand, Vol. III, pp. 615, 616.

[26] Melvin's "Judicial Bulwark," *ut ante,* pp. 185-193.

the record, there can be no doubt of what was intended by the 6th clause of the New Jersey Plan, until men engaged in a serious business do really use language to hide their meaning.

Little favor was, however, shown by the Convention to the New Jersey Plan, and the clause I have been considering was not even referred to. After no little debate, which was at times pointed enough, the plan as a whole was rejected on June 19, with only three negatives (New York, New Jersey, and Delaware), and the Randolph Plan, as reported from the Committee of the whole, was reported without change.[27]

The struggle in the Convention proper, as distinguished from the Committee of the whole, began now and was long and often acrimonious. It does not need to be much gone into here, and the next step of importance to us was the refusal of the Convention on July 17th, by three ayes to seven noes, to agree to the power of negativing the laws of the States, and so on.[28] The vote was a most serious defeat for the members who had in general theretofore directed the course of events, and must have seemed to them to leave the plan shorn of a chief and essential feature. They were, doubtless, for a time at a loss what next to do, and perhaps there was no little conversation out of order. If so, the debates are silent upon the subject, and their next record is the offer by Martin of (in effect) the 6th clause of the New Jersey Plan.[29] It was at once

[27] Farrand, Vol. I, p. 322.
[28] *Ibid.*, Vol. II, p. 28.
[29] It is of interest to know how Madison entered this resolution on his notes. He wrote out at first only his summation of

adopted *nem. con.*, without reported debate, and the Convention went on to other parts of the Constitution.

This clause, establishing the supremacy of the laws of the Union in the States and binding the State judiciaries to adhere to those laws in their decisions, despite contrary State laws, is the one that Martin wrote the next spring,—in his controversy with Ellsworth in the public papers,—he had offered *in substitution* of the plan of a general congressional negative, which he "considered totally inadmissible."[30]

Nor is evidence lacking that as leading a member as Madison, strongly opposed though he was to this plan, recognized much the same thing, and began at once to shape the Constitution in the way that the plan of judicial control would require. The very next day (July 18), he offered a clause in regard to the jurisdiction of the courts of the intended government, reading:

That the jurisdiction of the national Judiciary shall extend to cases arising under laws passed by the general

the substance, taking later from the "Journal" what now appears in the "Debates." Prof. Farrand wrote me on April 28, 1911, that Madison's original entry was in the following form: "that all the Legislative acts & Treaties made by virtue of the Articles of Union, shall be the supreme law of the States, and as such shall be observed by their Courts &c." See *ante*, pp. 132, 133.

[30] See Martin's letter of March 19, 1788, from the Maryland *Journal* reproduced in Farrand's "Records," Vol. III, pp. 286-295. Perhaps the present writer may be permitted to say that when, in 1899, he wrote in his "Growth of the Constitution" (p. 284) of Martin's proposal of July 17 as being "intended as a substitute for and to attain the same end as the clause which had just been defeated," he had no knowledge of this letter of Martin's. Farrand's "Records" had not then been published.

Legislature and to such other questions as involve the National peace and harmony.

This proposal was also unanimously adopted, apparently without debate.[31]

If there could be any doubt in regard to what the Convention was aiming at in all this matter, it is certainly removed by the debate of July 21, when Wilson again moved, and Madison seconded, a resolution that the National Judiciary "should be associated with the Executive in the Revisionary power." The proposal was discussed at some little length, Luther Martin objecting that it would give the Judges "a double negative," as the

constitutionality of laws . . . will come before the Judges in their proper official character [and] in this character they have a negative on the laws.

Mason answered Martin that, as the Constitution then stood, the Judiciary could only impede the operation of laws in one case,—when they were unconstitutional,—and he wished them to be able to prevent every improper law. Numbers of members spoke of the need of controlling the Legislature, or of establishing a "check" upon it against the passage of laws for paper money, the "remission of debts" or other "unjust measures," and the means they had in mind was the Judicial Department. The term "judicial control" had not yet come into vogue, and was not then used; but the idea was very plainly in the mind of Mason

[31] Farrand's "Records," Vol. II, p. 46; and see p. 39.

and others. And Mason at least wanted to extend this to the laws of the Central Power, as well as to those of the States. He thought it as necessary in the former case as in the latter.[32]

In all this matter, Martin was far from aiming at that broad power of control over State legislation which the Convention finally established. His wish was merely to make the supremacy extend to the *laws* of the States. Their constitutions were still to be paramount to the laws of Congress, and the whole matter was to be administered by the State Judiciary. He wanted no inferior Federal Courts.[33] He was accordingly opposed when; on July 18, power was conferred to create such tribunals; and evidently still more so, when the Convention went on and forged, blow by blow, that broad system of Federal supremacy which has almost completely curbed the States from violations of the rights of the Central Power in domestic as well as international relations.

Some writers of modern days have drawn the most remarkable conclusions from the rejection on July 17 of the plan of a Council of Revision, with the Judiciary forming a part of it. To them the action was the refusal to the Judiciary of power to hold a law unconstitutional. They probably did not know at the time they so wrote that Martin's proposal binding the State tribunals to follow in their decisions authorized Federal laws, despite contrary State ones, was ex-

[32] Farrand's "Records," Vol. II, pp. 73-80. Melvin's "Judicial Bulwark," etc., pp. 177-181.
[33] Letter in Farrand, Vol. III, pp. 286-295.

pressly said by him to have been offered *in substitution* for the proposal rejected, and they failed to observe certain other matters of a high degree of importance. Some few days after Martin's proposal had been agreed to, and when *the judicial method of curbing unauthorized State laws was thus in essence contained in the Constitution,* it has been seen that leading members (Wilson and Madison) none the less again moved on July 21 to add the Judiciary to the Executive in the revisionary power. And we shall find that the advocates of this general form of a Council of Revision did not even rest here, but twice again showed conclusively that they meant by this plan something quite different from the power to hold laws unconstitutional.

On July 26 the Convention referred all the resolutions they had agreed upon to a Committee of Detail, to draw up a Constitution in accordance therewith. One of the resolutions (the 7th) was Martin's proposal of July 17, while the 20th read

That the legislative, executive and judiciary powers, within the several states, and of the national government, ought to be bound, by oath, to support the Articles of Union.

Pinckney's plan and the New Jersey Plan were also referred.[34]

This Committee must have worked tirelessly, for their task was an arduous one, but on August 6 they reported a draft of a Constitution. In it was incorporated, almost in the same words, Martin's proposal

[34] Elliot's "Debates," Vol. V, pp. 375-376.

of July 17th as Article VIII, while the 20th resolution recited immediately above became Article XX. The powers of Congress were detailed in Article VII, and contained the well-known general clause "to make all laws that shall be necessary and proper for carrying into execution the foregoing powers," while Article XI, relating to the Judiciary, carried on the 16th resolution referred, by the provision (of vast moment in our discussion and showing plainly the understanding and the intent of the Committee of Detail) that "the jurisdiction of the Supreme Court shall extend to all cases arising under laws passed by the legislature of the United States."[35]

It sometimes happens that a proposal that never comes to maturity throws a very strong light on a complicated proceeding. So it was here, I think. Randolph's course in regard to the Constitution was by no means free from ground for criticism, but he was among the leading members, and very active. As one of the Committee of Detail, he drew up in his own handwriting a pretty complete outline of a form of Constitution, and in this he originally inserted, at the end of the clause detailing the Congressional powers, a provision that would alone show his intentions as to the function of the Judiciary in regard to unconstitutional laws but which, when coupled with his proposal earlier in the Convention,[36] leaves absolutely

[35] Elliot's "Debates," Vol. V, pp. 376-381.   Farrand, Vol. II, pp. 177-189.   The general words of the 16th resolution were defined and expanded, but what is quoted in the text contains the portions of moment here.
[36] *Ante*, pp. 130, 131.

no doubt as to them nor, I submit, as to their currency. As he wrote:

All laws of a particular State repugnant hereto shall be void; and in the decision thereon, which shall be vested in the supreme court, all incidents, without which the general principle cannot be satisfied, shall be considered as involved in the general principle.

And then, as if to show to a doubting later generation what he meant, he cancels these words and writes over them, "insert the eleventh article."[37] This was the article relating to the judicial power reported by the Committee of Detail, which expressly extended the jurisdiction of the Supreme Court "to all cases arising under laws passed by the legislature of the United States."

Hamilton, too, is plainly on record as having had Judicial Control in mind as a desideratum for us. Not only would his connection with Rutgers v. Waddington render this likely, but about the close of the Convention he communicated to Madison (not to the Convention) "a paper which he said delineated the Constitution which he would have wished to be proposed by the Convention: He had stated the principles of it in the course of the deliberations." [38] Article VII of this draft of a Constitution treated of the powers of the Legislature, and provided in its 6th clause that

[37] Farrand, Vol. II, p. 144. Meigs's "Growth of the Constitution," p. 285.
[38] Farrand, Vol. III, pp. 619-630.

the laws of the United States, and the treaties which have been made under the articles of the confederation, and which shall be made under this Constitution shall be the supreme law of the Land, and shall be so construed by the Courts of the several States.

But the advocates of a Council of Revision, with the Judiciary as a part of it, were not even at this late day satisfied; and though the plan reported provided plainly for the judicial annulment of unconstitutional State Laws, yet Madison once more, on August 15, moved an amendment embodying a Judicial Council of Revision, with the modification that the judges of the Supreme Court should separately consider all laws, and their separate assent be necessary as well as that of the Executive. The proposal was soon negatived by 3 ayes to 8 noes, but Gouverneur Morris wished that some such check could be agreed to, and suggested an absolute negative in the Executive. The Convention was, however, growing very impatient, and members complained of the endless delays.

There is some appearance, even after this, of a desire to adopt in part the wishes of Madison and his friends, and proposals were made and referred to the Committee of Detail for a Council of State, of which the Chief Justice should be part, and, again, that the Executive might require the opinion of the Supreme Court upon important matters. The Committee of Detail reported, too, on August 22 a clause to create a Privy Council, of which the Chief Justice of the Supreme Court should be one member; but the proposal was not carried out.[39]

All these efforts to bring the Judiciary in one way or another into the enactment of laws hence failed, and it is apparent that the Convention had finally settled itself upon the adoption of the Judicial method, by which the enforcement of laws of the States violating the Federal power was to be stopped by the Judiciary, after their enactment by the Legislatures. So the Convention did precisely what it was natural for the members to do under these circumstances. They went on to perfect the plan they had determined upon, precisely as it has already been seen [40] they had begun to do under the leadership of Madison on July 18. On August 23 Rutledge moved to amend the provision (then Article VIII, now Article VI, Clause 2) in regard to the supremacy of the laws of the Union, and the judges of the several States being bound thereby in their decisions, by prefixing the words "This Constitution and" to the words the laws of the United States, and so on, so that the provisions of the Constitution itself should equally be paramount to State laws. The amendment was agreed to *nem. con.*[41]

There remained one other clause of vital moment in this same connection. It was not enough to the legal confraternity to have provided that the United States Constitution and laws should be supreme. The juris-

[39] Farrand, Vol. II, pp. 328, 329, 341, 342, 367; or Elliot, Vol. V, pp. 442, 445, 446, 462.
[40] *Ante,* pp. 138, 139.
[41] Farrand, Vol. II, p. 389, or Elliot, Vol. V, p. 467.

diction of the courts must likewise be expressly so extended, in order to make the meaning perfectly clear and avoid the possibility of some over-refined distinction undoing what was intended. Therefore, when the clause concerning the jurisdiction of the Supreme Court (then Article XI, Section 3, now Article III, Section 2) came up on August 27, Dr. Johnson moved to insert here also the words "This Constitution and the" before the word "laws." It was plainly meant *ex majore cautela,* and to round out the instrument they were drafting, by expressly extending the jurisdiction of the courts to cover precisely the same ground to which the supremacy of the authority of the Union had already been extended, so that there should be a plain and palpable authorization to the Courts to hear and determine such cases. And, as if in order to make this intent still more clear, the debates tell us that Madison

doubted whether it was not going too far, to extend the jurisdiction of the court generally to cases arising under the Constitution, and whether it ought not to be limited to cases of a judiciary nature. The right of expounding the Constitution in cases not of this nature, ought not to be given to that department.

The motion of Dr. Johnson was agreed to *nem. con.,* it being generally supposed that the jurisdiction given was constructively limited to cases of a judiciary nature.[42]

Words could hardly be plainer, and particularly Madison's doubt and the reasons given for the unani-

[42] Farrand, Vol. II, p. 430.

mous action of the Convention show, beyond cavil, that the members then present had by this time come generally to realize that the system they were aiming to establish was intended to put upon the Judiciary the function of weeding out by their decisions at least all such laws of the States as should be found to be in violation of the Federal powers.

These two clauses (Article III, Section 2, and Article VI, Section 2, of the United States Constitution) were well called by Brinton Coxe [43] the "twin-texts" of the Constitution, and it was upon them that he relied to demonstrate,—in the portion of his work which he did not live to finish,—that the Constitution contains express texts providing for judicial competency · to decide questioned legislation to be constitutional or unconstitutional, and to hold it valid or void accordingly. That it does this, in so far as concerns legislation of the States in violation of the United States Constitution, is almost too plain for doubt, and there is the most persuasive evidence that it was equally meant to weed out unconstitutional congressional legislation.

In this connection, one fact is vital to be ever borne in mind: By this date a number of judicial decisions had been rendered in the States, holding void State laws which conflicted with their constitution, and these had been recognized and approved by men of note throughout the country to such an extent that, it may fairly be said, the principle was well advanced towards general acceptance. And this principle did

[43] "Judicial Power and Unconstitutional Legislation," "Introductory Note," pp. III-VIII.

not depend upon anything peculiar in the nature of the State governments, but extended in reason to the laws of any sovereignty,—at least, to all such as had a written constitution. These decisions were, moreover, known well enough to many leading members [44] of the Convention, and of course they passed this knowledge on to any of their colleagues who may have been less well informed. Such is the very purpose of discussion and debate.

And there is no lack of other evidence of their actual intentions. The proposals in Congress, in 1787, of what Brinton Coxe called "the identical law" was not a sudden outburst from a clear sky but the culmination of an effort to curb the States, which had been making in Congress since at least 1783. It cannot be doubted that Hamilton, Madison, and Ellsworth, who were of the Committee of Congress upon

[44] In my article of 1885 (*Amer. Law Review*, Vol. XIX, p. 184) I named Gerry, Gouverneur Morris, Sherman, Wilson, George Mason, and Luther Martin as commenting with approval upon the doctrine in the Convention, and Ellsworth, Davie, and Randolph, members of the Convention, as doing the same thing in the Ratifying Conventions. Since then this list has been greatly lengthened by Prof. Beard in his "Supreme Court and the Constitution," and in Mr. Melvin's "Judicial Bulwark of the Constitution" (*Amer. Polit. Science Review*, Vol. VIII, pp. 185-193). Mr. Melvin sums up: "of the fifty-five actual members of the federal convention some thirty-two to forty of them, that is two-thirds of the Convention and including nearly every influential member upheld or accepted the right of the courts," etc. I cannot but think that many of the names so included, are included on evidence of actions or opinions too much later in date, to prove that such was their opinion in 1787, but these gentlemen have added enough to my list,—all of leading or prominent men,—to make it formidable and far longer than I knew to be the case.

the subject in that year,[45] continued to watch the general subject, and when the Courts of the States began of their own accord to make decisions holding void State laws that violated the Federal authority, they or some of their colleagues doubtless suggested that application of these decisions which was molded into the proposed identical law. This law was recommended at a meeting of Congress, when all the States except New Hampshire were present, and when Rhode Island was represented by Varnum, of Trevett *v.* Weeden. It received the votes of King, Johnson, Madison, Blount, Few and Pierce,—all members of the coming Convention.[46]

In regard to Madison's understanding that the Convention intended to adopt the Judicial Method of voiding unauthorized State laws, the evidence is absolutely overwhelming. He was disappointed at the refusal to adopt the Council of Revision plan, with power to veto State laws *in limine,* and wrote to Jefferson almost contemporaneously (October 24, 1787), that

It may be said that the Judicial authority, under our new system, will keep the States within their proper limits, and supply the place of a negative on their laws. The answer is, that it is more convenient to prevent the passage of a law than to declare it void after it is passed.[47]

And again in the Virginia Ratifying Convention, he used language showing plainly the same understand-

[45] *Ante,* p. 92.
[46] Melvin's "Judicial Bulwark," etc., pp. 173, 174.
[47] Farrand, Vol. III, pp. 131-136. See *ante,* pp. 128, 129.

ing, that the Judiciary were to curb the States from violating the federal powers.[48]

His reminiscences in later life are, if possible, even clearer and to precisely the same effect. Perhaps, the most conclusive is contained in his letter of 1831 to N. P. Trist, in which he wrote:

The obvious necessity of a control on the laws of the States, so far as they might violate the constitution and laws of the United States, left no option but as to the mode. The modes presenting themselves, were (1) a veto on the passage of the State laws. (2) A Congressional repeal of them. (3) A Judicial annulment of them. The 1st though extensively favored, at the outset, was found on discussion, liable to insuperable objections, arising from the extent of the Country and the multiplicity of State laws. The 2d was not free from such as gave a preference to the third as now provided by the Constitution.[49]

When so leading a man as Madison, whose favorite idea in the matter had been defeated, wrote in this way of the action of the Convention,—and when we remember the crying need of a means to annul State laws in violation of the Federal authorities, as well as the course of the Convention in the connection, and

[48] Elliot, Vol. III, p. 532.
[49] Farrand's "Records," Vol. III, pp. 516, 517. See also the same ideas expressed in other words in letter of October 21, 1833, to W. C. Rives, *ibid.*, pp. 521-524, and in his "Introduction to the Debates," *ibid.*, pp. 539, *etc.*, where he writes that "instead of the proposed negative, the objects of it were left as finally provided for in the constitution."

the opinions of other men of great prominence,[50]—
it is not possible to doubt that the "Judicial Method"
was definitely adopted by the Framers for this purpose.

But this was not all. What of laws of Congress
unauthorized by the terms of the Constitution? Can
it be supposed for a moment that those very careful
men forgot this point, or actually meant to leave each
Congress free in its uncontrolled discretion to interpret
the instrument to mean what that body might at the
moment think expedient? If any one believes this
possible, he can have little knowledge of the jealousy
of power which was then almost universally prevalent.
Had the Constitution been supposed to carry this
meaning, there can be no shadow of doubt but that
the smaller States would all have instantly rejected
the instrument, rather than submit themselves to the
absolute power of the larger States. The possibility
of this interpretation was seen to some extent, and the
fear of it was one cause of alarm, but the many answers made in the *Federalist* and other publications,
as well as in the Ratifying Conventions, were in general apparently found satisfactory.

The subject might almost be left here, as it seems
to me, and the intent that the judicial power should
extend also to laws of Congress unauthorized by the
Constitution, be rested on general inference from the
surrounding circumstances,—the wide recognition of
the like power throughout the States, the long and
painful labor devoted to defining the powers, the fre-

[50] See, for example, Randolph's and Hamilton's proposals,
ante, pp. 130, 142-144.

quent insertion of clauses that specific things should not be done by the proposed Government, the putting of all these provisions in the intended treble strong brass of a permanent writing, the creation of great and independent Departments of Government bound by solemn oath to obey the Constitution, and the palpable fact that without some means of curbing Congress, sure to be often swept from its anchorage by wild gusts of popular passion, the deepest discontents would soon prevail in many parts of the country, and the new experiment end ere long in blood, failure, and revolution.

But some writers of modern days by no means admit this general view; and it is hence necessary to follow the subject further and see what other evidence of the intent can be found.

The Constitution was to be the supreme law of the land, but this supremacy was only extended to such of the laws of Congress as should be made *in pursuance* thereof. As Hamilton had put it in No. 33 (31) of the *Federalist*:

> It will not follow from this doctrine that acts of the larger society which are *not pursuant* to its constitutional powers, . . . will become the supreme law of the land. . . . It [the constitution] *expressly* confines this supremacy to laws made *pursuant to the constitution*.

And Madison wrote in No. 44 (43) of the same great commentary that, if Congress should misconstrue their authority to pass laws necessary and proper, the result would be the same as if they should misconstrue or enlarge any other power vested in them . . . *the same in short as if the State Legislatures should violate their respective constitutional authorities.*[51] In the first instance, the success of the usurpation will depend on the executive and judiciary departments which are to expound and give effect to the legislative acts.

To the same effect, the future great Chief Justice said in the Virginia Ratifying Convention,[52]

Can they go beyond the delegated powers? If they were to make a law not warranted by any of the powers enumerated, it would be considered by the judges as an infringement of the Constitution which they are to guard. They would not consider such a law as coming under their jurisdiction. They would declare it void. . . . To what quarter will you look for protection from an infringement of the Constitution, if you will not give the power to the judiciary. There is no other power that can afford such a protection.

Iredell, too, wrote to precisely the same effect in 1787, "It really appears to me, the exercise of the power [by the Judiciary] is unavoidable, the Constitution not being a mere imaginary thing." [53]

[51] Italics mine.
[52] Elliot, Vol. III, p. 553. It is interesting to remember that Marshall had studied law with Wythe, who took part in Comm. *v.* Caton in 1782, and wrote in his opinion: "Nay, more, if the whole Legislature" should attempt to overleap the bounds prescribed by the Constitution, he would meet them from his seat and say "hither shall you go, but no further." See *ante,* p. 64.
[53] Reply to letter of Spaight strongly criticising the decision in Bayard *v.* Singleton, quoted more at length, *ante,* p. 121.

It has been said that it was fairly well established by this time in the States, that a law violating the State Constitution was void, and would be so held by their Courts. And not only was the analogy of like laws of Congress violating the United States Constitution perfect, but the need for a cure was perhaps even stronger in the latter case, for such an unauthorized law would otherwise violate the rights of thirteen States. If a written Constitution, with all its so laboriously drawn authorities and limitations, was not to be from the start a vain thing, with no defense against the encroachments of Power, which the men of that day so much feared, some method must be found in the system to protect the instrument from such violations; and Marshall, Madison, Hamilton, and Iredell have all been shown to have pointed out,—before the Constitution went into effect,—the Judicial Department as the one to exercise this function.

In addition to all this contemporaneous evidence, it is curious to find that in a very few years, when the general subject was discussed at the time of the Pension Cases, it was pointed out [54] that, unless our Courts were to exercise the power in question, there was no agency in our system, short of a Constitutional Convention, that could prevent the carrying out of unconstitutional laws.

Calhoun, too, who fully believed in the general power of the courts as to unconstitutional laws, while rejecting some of its apparent results or derivatives, said much the same thing in other words many years

[54] *The Philadelphia Aurora,* of April 20, 1792, quoted *post,* p. 182.

later. In his speech of February 15 and 16, 1833, on the Force Bill, made in the Senate when the contest over Nullification was still most acute, after first denying that the power was conferred upon the Supreme Court by the Constitution, he said:

I do not deny that it possesses the right; but I can by no means concede that it was derived from the Constitution. It had its origin in the necessity of the case. Where there are two or more rules established, one from a higher, the other from a lower authority, which may come into conflict in applying them to a particular case, the judge cannot avoid pronouncing in favor of the superior against the inferior.[55]

Again, in the treatment of the general subject by the Convention, the laws of Congress were coupled in the same clause with the laws of the States, and the same result would hence naturally follow as to both. In-

[55] "Works," Vol. II, pp. 201-203. Some writers have thought very differently of Calhoun's opinions on this subject, but they have probably been misled by his refusal to admit that a State could be concluded, as to the meaning of the constitution, by a decision of the Supreme Court in an ordinary case between parties. He would doubtless also have denied, with the State Rights School in general, the right to an appeal to the Supreme Court in any case in which a State was a party. The decision of the federal courts in some question arising under Nullification, might have been very inconvenient to the South Carolina leaders, and at the session of 1830-31 Warren R. Davis (a close political friend of Calhoun) moved to repeal that portion of the Judiciary Act of 1789, which gives a right of appeal to the Supreme Court of the United States from the decree of a State Supreme Court,—but which had always been opposed by the ultra State Rights School. The motion was lost, but was hardly made without Calhoun's consent, despite the fact that he thought it went very much beyond Nullification, "Life of Calhoun," by William M. Meigs, Vol. I, pp. 420, 421.

deed, Madison has been just shown to have said (absolutely assuming the voidness of State laws in violation of the State Constitution) that, if Congress should exceed its authority and pass unauthorized laws, the same result would follow as did when the State Legislatures violated their constitution. That the invalidity of unauthorized laws was made plainer in the new instrument,—and indeed absolutely plain as to State laws which should violate the United States Constitution,—was owing to the fact that such unauthorized State laws and their avoidance constituted one of the chief points of importance in the minds of the Framers, and had been a large factor in leading to the Convention.

But the adoption of the Judicial Method even as to these State laws could hardly possibly have been thought of had not the judges in a number of States already laid down the general principle that a law in violation of a written constitution was void, and would be so held by the Courts of the particular jurisdiction in a judicial case brought before them. This great principle was used by the Convention to attain their end as to State laws unauthorized under the Federal Constitution; but it had precisely the same application to laws of Congress unauthorized under the new Constitution as it had to the laws of one of our States unauthorized under its Constitution.

The Convention then enacted, in the plainest words, the specific point that State laws in violation of the Federal functions were to be held void by the Courts, thus using the new principle to get rid of offending

State laws, but it left a little to inference from the well-known growth of Judicial Power in our country as to Unconstitutional Legislation, the other point that unauthorized laws of Congress should (to paraphrase Madison's language quoted above) meet with the same treatment as did those of the State Legislatures when they violated their respective constitutional authorities.

CHAPTER VIII

THE CONSTITUTION BEFORE THE PEOPLE, AND IN THE RATIFYING CONVENTIONS

THE term "Judicial Power" has been used by the writer in the preceding chapter with reference to its adoption by the Convention as the means of stopping unconstitutional laws. It is a term that was not used in that sense at the time, so far as I know; but the idea is plainly to be found in speeches in the Convention, and in the *Federalist* and other writings of leading men at about that date. The idea was already becoming formulated, or integrated, and was in time crystallized in that expression. Madison has been shown to have used in several instances language that plainly imported this power, and Hamilton did the same thing in No. 78 and other numbers of the *Federalist*.

Many writers have said with truth that a point of first importance in interpreting the Constitution is to find out what the Ratifying Conventions understood any disputed clause to mean; for it was their action that breathed life into the instrument. As to many such clauses, there is, of course, great doubt; portions of the instrument have ever been differently understood by different writers; but in relation to the intended power of the Judiciary under the new system to hold unconstitutional State laws violating the Federal authorities, it is difficult to see how there can be any question.

And the same right applies to laws of Congress unauthorized by the new Constitution, only less clearly. The laws of Congress and those of the States were always treated together by the Convention, without any difference being drawn between them in this respect; and before the people the burden of the discussions related to unauthorized laws of Congress, for one of the dreads of opponents was that the powers of Congress would be indefinitely extended, both by the legislative authority under the new system, and by the favoring interpretation of such extensions by the Federal Courts, while the advocates of the new system put their reliance on an honest Federal Judiciary, which would interpret the new system with fairness.

Little, if anything, new can be written to-day about the discussion of the Constitution in 1787 and 1788, and the intention of the writer in the present chapter is to present shortly some of the public utterances upon this subject by the essayists of the day and in the Ratifying Conventions, leaving to already existing writings the full details of this branch of the subject. Enough will, I think, be produced to show conclusively that the Judicial Power was most widely recognized, and its great influence understood, both by friend and foe of the new system. Friends lauded it, as sure to result in holding the new system within bounds, while foes denounced it, as destined to render the Central

System absolute, and utterly to abrogate the powers and rights of the States. Both classes of commentators will, of course, be cited here, for the evidence of the one is as strong as that of the other in regard to the belief in the existence in the Constitution of the Judicial Power.

It should be added that, so far as I know, the existence of the power was nowhere denied by any writer of repute. Some, doubtless, still thought it an unwise power to have conferred, but not one seems to have expressed doubt as to the intention of the Convention to incorporate it in the new Constitution.

Hardly had the Constitutional Convention adjourned, when Pierce Butler, a member from South Carolina, wrote (October 8) a letter detailing some items of the plan, and specifying that they had agreed upon "a Judiciary to be Supreme in all matters relating to the General Government, and Appellate in State Controversies." [1]

And the "Remarks to the People of Maryland" by Aristides,[2]—who was Alexander Contee Hanson, a member of the Maryland State Convention, and Chancellor of the State from 1789 until his death,—are very plain on this point, touching, however, on other matters as well. He writes of the clause as to making any laws which shall be necessary and proper, and then refers to the apprehension that this "sweeping clause"

[1] Farrand's "Records," Vol. III, pp. 102, 103.
[2] Paul Leicester Ford's "Pamphlets on the Constitution of the United States published during its discussion by the People, 1787-1788," pp. 217-257.

will afford a pretext for freeing Congress from all constitutional restraints, going on to say:

I take the construction of these words to be precisely the same as if the clause had preceded [*sic*] further and said, "No Act of Congress shall be valid, unless it have relation to the foregoing powers, and be necessary and proper for carrying them into execution." But say the objectors, "The Congress, being of itself to judge of the necessity and propriety, may pass any act, which it may deem *expedient,* for any other purpose." This objection applies with equal force to each particular power defined by the Constitution. . . . They may reflect, however, that every judge in the Union, whether of State or federal appointment (and some persons would say every jury[3]) will have a right to reject any act handed to him as a law, which he may conceive repugnant to the Constitution.

Elbridge Gerry, in his "Observations," [4] was far less favorable, and went into many objections, the following among others:

There are no well defined limits of the Judiciary Powers, they seem to be left as a boundless ocean, that has broken over the chart of the Supreme Lawgiver, "thus far shalt thou go and no further," and as they cannot be comprehended by the clearest capacity or the most sagacious mind, it would be a Herculean labor to attempt to describe the dangers with which they are replete.

[3] This seems to us to-day a curious idea; but it was evidently not confined to Hanson's mind, for Luther Martin argued against it upon the trial of the impeachment of Judge Chase in 1804, Farrand's "Records," Vol. III, pp. 407, 408.
[4] Ford's "Pamphlets," *etc.,* p. 9.

Robert Yates of New York, as "Brutus," was very clear as to the broad powers conferred on the Judiciary and very decidedly against this part of the Constitution. As he wrote in one of his papers:

This Government is a complete system, not only for making, but for executing laws. And the courts of law, which will be constituted by it, are not only to decide on the Constitution and laws made in pursuance of it, but by officers subordinate to them, to execute all their decisions. . . . No errors they may commit can be corrected by any power above them, if any such power there be, nor can they be removed from office for making ever so many erroneous decisions. . . . The opinions of the Supreme Court, whatever they may be, will have the force of law; because there is no power provided in the Constitution, that can correct their errors or control their jurisdiction. From this court there is no appeal. And I conceive the legislature themselves cannot set aside a decree of this court, because they are authorized by the Constitution to decide in the last resort. [And in a later number he added] The supreme court then have a right, independent of the legislature, to give a construction to the Constitution and every part of it, and there is no power provided in this system to correct their construction or do away with it. If therefore the legislature pass any laws inconsistent with the sense the judges put upon the Constitution, they will declare it void.[5]

In the *Federalist*, the treatise which may almost be said to have been published by authority, the right and

[5] Quoted in Davis's "Annulment of Legislation by the Supreme Court" in *Amer. Polit. Sci. Rev.*, Vol. VII, p. 577, from Paul Leicester Ford's "Essays on the Constitution of the United States," etc., p. 295.

duty of the Judiciary in regard to unconstitutional laws were recognized and asserted in numbers of the papers, some of which have already been quoted in these pages, but the following may be added. In Number XVI, referring to an invasion of National rights by the State Legislature, Hamilton writes:

If the judges were not embarked in a conspiracy with the legislature, they would pronounce the resolutions of such a majority to be contrary to the supreme law of the land, unconstitutional and void.

And his exclusion from the supremacy, provided by the Constitution, of laws of Congress not passed in pursuance of the instrument [6] is equally clear. In a late number (LXXX) he examined the question whether the limitations were merely binding on the consciences of members of Congress, and hence what lawyers call "directory"; but his conclusion was that they are far more than this, and are mandatory.[7]

The acrid Luther Martin, who had been so closely concerned with the early beginnings of the provisions as to Judicial Power, but whose limited ideas upon the subject had been entirely overruled, in his lengthy "Genuine Information," told the Maryland Legislature on November 29, 1787, that

whether, therefore, any *laws* or *regulations* of the Congress, or any *acts* of its *President* or *other officers,* are

[6] *Ante,* p. 152.
[7] Those who desire to follow further the opinions expressed by the *Federalist* should consult Nos. XVI, XXXIII, LXXVIII, LXXIX, and LXXX.

contrary to, or *warranted* by the constitution, rests only with the judges, who are *appointed* by Congress to determine; by whose determination *every State* must be bound.[8]

In Pennsylvania, the unknown author of "Centinel" argued as follows against the Constitution in his Number V, and after quoting Article VI in regard to the Constitution and laws, etc., being supreme, wrote:

The words "pursuant to the constitution" will be no restriction to the authority of Congress; for the foregoing sections give them unlimited jurisdiction; their unbounded power of taxation alone includes all others, as whoever has the purse-strings will have full dominion. . . . [But the Convention has added also the power to make all laws necessary and proper.] Whatever law Congress may deem necessary and proper for carrying into execution any of the powers vested in them may be enacted; and by virtue of this clause, they may control and abrogate any and every law of the State governments, on the allegation that they interfere with the execution of any of their powers. . . . [And in a later Number (XVI) he argues to much the same effect, and adds that the laws would be subject to the scrutiny of the judges] whose province it would be to determine the constitutionality of any law that may be controverted.[9]

In the debates in the Pennsylvania Ratifying Convention, the general subject was most clearly stated

[8] Farrand's "Records," Vol. III, pp. 172-230: see especially p. 220.
[9] "Centinel" is reproduced in "Pennsylvania and the Federal Convention," edited by John Bach McMaster and Frederick D. Stone, pp. 611, 612, 659.

by at least two members. Wilson's views are so well known that it is almost surplusage to reproduce them, but the following is so plain as to be worth the space it will take:

I say, under this constitution, the legislature may be restrained and kept within its prescribed bounds by the interposition of the judicial department. [Should the Legislature transgress the bounds assigned to it and pass an unauthorized law], when it comes to be discussed before the judges, when they consider its principles and find it to be incompatible with the superior powers of the constitution, it is their duty to pronounce it void; and judges independent, and not obliged to look every session for a continuance of their salaries, will behave with intrepidity and refuse to the act the sanction of judicial authority.[10]

And Wilson reports McKean as saying similarly of the Legislature that

It may be restrained in several ways:
1. By the judges deciding against the Legislature in Favor of the Constitution.[11]

Fears were expressed in the Ratifying Conventions of at least two States that the restrictions contained

[10] *Ibid.*, pp. 304-305, and see the same thing expressed again later at p. 340 and p. 354. Immediately after the matter quoted in the text, Wilson goes on: "In the same manner, the President of the United States could shield himself and refuse to carry into effect an act that violates the Constitution"; see also pp. 305 and 398. I shall return to this again in the last chapter of this book.
[11] *Ibid.*, p. 766.

in the Constitution would be overridden by Congress, and the powers be enormously extended. In Massachusetts these objections were met by the recommendation in the resolution of ratification of amendments, one of which contained the clause that "all powers not expressly delegated . . . were reserved," etc. This brought from Sam Adams the following statement:

It removes a doubt which many have entertained respecting the matter and gives assurance that, if any law made by the federal government shall be extended beyond the powers granted by the proposed Constitution, and inconsistent with the constitution of this state, it will be an error, and adjudged by the courts of law to be void.[12]

In the New York Convention, Williams and Melancthon Smith thought the powers conferred gave Congress express authority to pass any law they might please and might judge necessary; Smith even specifying that

they would have power to abrogate the laws of the States, and to prevent the operation of their taxes; and all courts, before whom any dispute on these points should come, whether federal or not, would be bound by oath to give judgment according to the laws of the Union.

Similarly, Williams referred to the language as to providing for the common defense and general welfare, and that in regard to passing necessary and proper laws, continuing thus:

[12] Elliot's "Debates," Vol. II, pp. 122, 123, 131, 177, 178.

It is, therefore, evident that the legislature, under this constitution, may pass any law which they may think proper. [And added later] If the Congress should judge it a proper provision for the common defense and general welfare that the state governments should be essentially destroyed, what, in the name of common sense, will prevent them? Are they not constitutionally authorized to pass such laws? [13]

Nothing could be plainer than Ellsworth's expressions in the Connecticut Ratifying Convention, when he said:

This Constitution defines the extent of the powers of the general government. If the general legislature should at any time overleap their limits, the judicial department is a constitutional check. If the United States go beyond their powers, if they make a law which the Constitution does not authorize, it is void; and the judicial powers, the national judges, who, to secure their impartiality, are to be made independent, will declare it to be void. On the other hand, if the States go beyond their limits, if they make a law which is a usurpation upon the general government, the law is void; and upright, independent judges will declare it so. [14]

From the debates of the Virginia Convention Marshall has already been quoted [15] as most distinctly asserting the power of the Judiciary, while Patrick Henry said: [16]

[13] *Ibid.*, pp. 330, 334, 338, 378.
[14] Farrand's "Records," Vol. III, pp. 240, 241.
[15] *Ante*, p. 153.
[16] Elliot's "Debates," Vol. III, pp. 324, 325.

Yes, sir, our judges opposed the acts of the legislature. We have this landmark to guide us. They had fortitude to declare that they were the judiciary, and would oppose unconstitutional acts. Are you sure that your federal judiciary will act thus?

To the opinions already quoted might be added like ones from numbers of others, too,—Grayson, Pendleton, and Randolph in Virginia; in Delaware, Dickinson; in New York, Hamilton and others; in South Carolina, Rutledge, and C. C. Pinckney, and in North Carolina, Steele, Davie, and Iredell [17] whose opinions have already been shown in these pages. Baldwin, of far-off Georgia, was also a believer in the general doctrine.[18]   But more than enough recognition of the existence of the Judicial Power in the new system has been cited, until some denials that it had any place in it are shown us from somewhere.

During the time while the Constitution was under consideration in the States, or a little later, and at least before it was put into operation, the question came up twice judicially in separate States,—in Virginia in the case of the Judges, and in South Carolina in Ham v. McClaws. In the first-named case,[19] in 1788, the Court of Appeals and other courts of Virginia sent a remonstrance to the Legislature against a recent statute requiring them, in addition to their

[17] Melvin's "Judicial Bulwark," *Amer. Polit. Sci. Rev.*, Vol. VIII, p. 198.   For Steele, Horace A. Davis's "Annulment of Legislation by the Supreme Court," *ibid.*, Vol. VII, p. 579, citing Elliot's "Debates," Vol. IV, p. 71.

[18] Davis's "Annulment," etc., *ibid.*, p. 555.

[19] 4 Call's Reports, 135.

existing duties, to act as judges of a newly established District Court, without increase of salary. They declined to do as required, saying that the act was contrary to the Constitution, and therefore must be controlled by the Constitution. The subject remained a matter of controversy, and was again under judicial consideration in Kamper v. Hawkins in 1793, when the judges were unanimous that the law was unconstitutional. In the end the act was amended, and the judges all resigned, but requalified under the new statute.[20]

In Ham v. McClaws [21] in 1789, the Superior Court of South Carolina not only wrote that "it is clear, that statutes passed against the plain and obvious principles of common right, and common reason, are absolutely null and void, as far as they are calculated to operate against those principles," but held that an act of 1788, which positively and without exception prohibited the importation of negroes, did not apply to an actual settler, who had made such importation under a prior act of 1787 and could not possibly have known, at the time of his importation, of the act of 1788. The case was, it is true, put upon the basis of interpretation, and that they would not do the Legislature the injustice to suppose that such a result was intended; but it went a long way in interpretation, and the tendency was plainly in the direction of holding laws void in some cases.

[20] Kamper v. Hawkins, 2 Va. Cases (Brockenbrough and Holmes), 20.
[21] 1 Bay, 93.

CHAPTER IX

WHEN once the Constitution went into effect, in 1789, it was to be expected, after all that had been said in public by that date of its meaning in regard to the Judiciary, that that department's powers under the new instrument would be widely asserted and recognized throughout the country. And such was the case. From many sources, some of such a character as to be utterly unanswerable, came up rapidly year by year a mass of proof.

In the very first Congress, where as many of the Framers as eighteen,—that is, fully one-third,—sate as members,[1] and had that leading-hand in legislation which belonged of right to them, one really conclusive evidence of the meaning of the instrument in regard to the Judiciary was quickly furnished. Numbers of Acts of Congress were required to put the new Government into operation and to bring into play the various provisions of the Constitution. One of these new laws was the Judiciary Act of September 24, 1789, which has stood the test of years so well that many of its provisions are still to-day in effect. It is well known to have been drawn by Ellsworth of Connecticut,

[1] Melvin's "Judicial Bulwark," *ut ante,* p. 200.

whose course in the Federal Convention,—and still more in the Connecticut Ratifying Convention,—can leave no shadow of doubt as to his belief in the power of the Judiciary to hold laws (either of the United States or of the States) unconstitutional in a proper case. With him on the committee were Paterson, Few, Strong, and Bassett,—all likewise Framers.[2]

By one clause of the Act of 1789,[3] appellate jurisdiction was conferred upon the United States Supreme Court from any decree in a case in the proper State or Federal Court in which a statute or treaty of the United States had been called in question, and the decision had been *against* its validity. That is to say, not only was it recognized that the State Courts and the lower Courts of the United States might perhaps hold statutes of a State to be in violation of the United States Constitution, and hence void, but that they would probably at times hold a State statute valid and a Federal statute conflicting with it void, because of the latter's not being authorized under the Constitution; or in other words, as the *Federalist* had put it, because the Federal statute was *not* passed *in pursuance of* the Constitution.

Nor is this all: full power was conferred in these cases on the United States Supreme Court in error.

[2] On the origin of the Judiciary Act, see Madison, May 30, 1832, to Edward Everett, in "Works," by Congress, 1865, Vol. IV, pp. 220, 221: "Life of Ellsworth," by Henry Flanders, in "Lives and Times of the Chief Justices," Vol. II, p. 159: Davis's "Annulment," etc., *ut ante.*, p. 546: Melvin's "Judicial Bulwark," *ut ante.*, p. 200.

[3] Story's "Statutes of the United States" (2d edition, by Geo. Sharswood), p. 53. Sec. 25 is the section in question.

It could either affirm or reverse, and must do the one or the other. If it affirms a ruling of the lower court against the power claimed under the United States Constitution or law, it must first inquire and must decide for itself that the Federal law is unconstitutional and void,—or, if it thinks the Federal law to be in pursuance of the Constitution and the conflicting State law void, it must so find, and therefore reverse. The final decision is ever a decision of the Supreme Court. The only limitation is that, if the lower court has decreed in favor of the power claimed for the United States, there is no right at all of error or appeal, for the evident reason that the power has then been already recognized. However, where an appeal, or error, does lie, the United States Supreme Court must distinctly rule (if it affirms) that a Federal statute is unauthorized and void. This seems to have been questioned,[4] but surely nothing could be plainer on examination; nor does it seem possible to doubt that such was the intention of Ellsworth and of whoever aided him in drafting the Act, and of the Members of Congress who passed it. They evidently designed to give the Supreme Court the right to interpret the Federal Constitution, and the power to reverse (and equally to affirm) any decree of a lower court *against* a Federal power fully secured this end.

It is worthy of mention, too, that, in a course of lectures delivered at the College of Philadelphia in

[4] Horace A. Davis's "Annulment of Legislation," *ut ante.*, pp. 583 *et seq.* See Mr. Melvin's answer in his "Judicial Bulwark," *ut ante.*

1790-91,[5] James Wilson reasserted his already expressed views on the subject, and that in 1802 Judge Tucker maintained similar views in his edition of Blackstone;[6] so that the doctrine was soon being taught and spread far and wide among students and the oncoming generation. When, too, Elias Boudinot was warned in the House of Representatives, in 1791, that the Courts would decide the proposed Bank of the United States to be unconstitutional, he not only referred to the right of the Judiciary, but openly expressed his boast and confidence therein.[7]

Soon, too, more judicial decisions recognizing and exercising the power began to appear. In 1791, New Hampshire,—which had already heard the doctrine asserted in her Legislature and probably in her lower Courts,[8]—definitely joined the column of States in which the power of the courts was enforced by the Judiciary.

One Elizabeth McClary had lost a suit in Rockingham County, and, in accordance with what has been shown [9] to have been a practice,—often roundly stopped by the King in Council in colonial days,—she then petitioned the Legislature in 1790 and secured the passage of "an act to restore [her] to her rights." In other words, the Legislature undertook to interfere with the Judiciary, and to grant a new trial in a case

[5] "Lectures on Law," by James Wilson, Vol. I, pp. 460, 461.
[6] Tucker's "Blackstone," Vol. I, Appendix, pp. 354, 355.
[7] Benton's "Abridgment," Vol. I, p. 291.
[8] *Ante*, pp. 73, 74.
[9] *Ante*, pp. 74, 75.

already determined.   On the new trial, counsel for the original plaintiff objected

that the act could not entitle the original defendant to a trial by way of appeal, for if it reversed the judgment, it was repugnant to the constitution of the State: and if it did not reverse the judgment, the same might be pleaded in bar.

After a full hearing, the Court entered the following decree:

It appears to the court that if the act virtually or really reverses the judgment of this court, it is repugnant to the bill of rights and constitution of this State, and if the Act does not reverse the said judgment the court cannot render another judgment in the same case upon appeal, while the first judgment remains in full force.   It is therefore considered by the Court that the said Act is ineffectual and inadmissible, and that the said action be dismissed.

The case was in the Superior Court for the County of Rockingham.[10]

[10] See article by Walter F. Dodd in *Amer. Histor. Rev.*, Vol. XII, pp. 348-350. Mr. Dodd examined the MS. Records of the two houses of the Legislature of New Hampshire, and of the Superior Court for Rockingham County, for Sept., 1791, and the quotations in my text are from these original authorities cited by him.   See also William Plumer's "Life of Wm. Plumer," pp. 170-172 and 59, and my article in Vol. XLVII of the *Amer. Law Review*, p. 683, *etc.* It will be observed how exactly what Plumer writes of his father's contentions in the case agrees with the original records found by Mr. Dodd. When I wrote my article, it is needless to say that I did not know the subject had been so much more thoroughly studied by Mr. Dodd several years before.

In 1792, in Bowman *v.* Middleton,[11] and again in 1805 in White *v.* Kendrick,[12] South Carolina followed the indications of Ham *v.* McClaws,[13] and aligned herself far more fully with the growing doctrine in regard to Judicial Power. In the case of 1792, a law of 1712 was held void, which aimed to vest the title to land in certain persons without a trial by jury or otherwise, the Court saying that the law was "against common right, as well as against *magna charta.*" And the decision of 1805 held void a law of 1801, extending the jurisdiction of justices of the peace to cases involving as much as $30, for the reason that it violated a provision of the Constitution that trial by jury should remain as theretofore, and justices had never had jurisdiction to so large an amount.

In 1792 and 1793 Virginia again rendered decisions of importance in the matter. Turner *v.* Turner [14] was perhaps in the main a question of the proper interpretation of an Act of Assembly; but Page *v.* Pendleton [15] very distinctly ruled that a debt due to a British creditor was not discharged by payment in paper money into the loan office, under the Act of 1788, despite the fact that this statute expressly enacted that it should be; and in Kamper *v.* Hawkins [16] the General Court held unanimously that the Judges were not bound by a

[11] I Bay, 252.
[12] I Brevard, 469.
[13] *Ante,* p. 169.
[14] 4 Call, 234.
[15] 4 Wythe, 211.
[16] 2 Va. Cases (Brockenbrough and Holmes), 20. This case has been already mentioned, *ante,* p. 169.

statute which required them to sit also as members of a newly-created court, without additional pay.

New Jersey, too, was heard from again in 1796, when, in Taylor *v.* Reading,[17] her Supreme Court reasserted the ruling of Holmes *v.* Walton [18] in 1780; and she ruled the same way once more in 1804, in State *v.* Parkhurst,[19] after a very determined contest. North Carolina adhered to Bayard *v.* Singleton in Ogden *v.* Witherspoon [20] in 1802, and in University *v.* Foy [21] in 1805.

During about this same period two more States ranged themselves clearly enough, for the first time, on the side of the Judiciary's power: Pennsylvania in Austin *v.* Trustees [22] in 1793, and in Respublica *v.* Duquet [23] in 1799, and Maryland in 1802 in Whittington *v.* Polk.[24] In Austin *v.* Trustees, there was another ground for the decision; but the Supreme Court of Pennsylvania expressed itself as having "no difficulty in declaring . . . that the former act was *unconstitutional*": while in the Duquet case, so far had the doctrine in general come to be accepted, that Jared Ingersoll, a leader of the bar and member of the Federal Convention, divided his argument into two heads, the first of which was: "Is the law of . . . unconstitutional?"; and the Court wrote in its opinion

---

[17] 4 Halstead, Appendix, 444.
[18] See *ante,* pp. 61-63.
[19] 4 Halstead, Appendix, 444.
[20] 2 Haywood, 227 or 404.
[21] 1 Murphy, 58.
[22] 1 Yeates, 260.
[23] 2 Yeates, 493.
[24] 1 Harris & Johnson, 236.

that, though there was no breach of the Constitution shown in the case, and though the breach must be very plain before they would hold a law void,

> Yet if a violation of the constitution should in any case be made by an act of the legislature, and that violation should unequivocally appear to us, we shall think it our duty not to shrink from the task of saying such law is void.

In Whittington v. Polk, though the act in question was held not to be unconstitutional, both sides admitted that an act of assembly repugnant to the Constitution was void, and that the Court had the right so to determine. The opinion added that these points "have not been controverted in any of the cases which have been brought before this court."

Before the end of the eighteenth century, therefore, there were no less than eight cases in as many States,— New Jersey, Connecticut, Rhode Island, North Carolina, South Carolina, New Hampshire, Virginia, and Pennsylvania, i.e., nearly two-thirds of all,—enforcing the right of the Judiciary to refuse to carry out a statute on the ground of its unconstitutionality; and with these New York may almost be joined, while Maryland has just been shown to have tended most strongly in the same direction in 1802.[25] In 1801, the new State of Kentucky ruled to precisely the same effect in Stidger v. Rogers.[26]

Nor is even this by any means all the evidence fur-

[25] Cf. with pp. 121-123.
[26] See *ante,* p. 76.

nished by these first few years of the new Government's existence, when the Framers were still easily in control of affairs. A potent voice had come up from the Federal Courts as well. The question first arose in them in cases relating to Pensions. Congress had passed on March 23, 1792,[27] a statute directing the circuit court judges to hear petitions of applicants to be placed on the pension-lists, and the decrees in such cases were to be subject to suspension by the Secretary of War and to revision by Congress. At least four of the Circuit Courts demurred, and one of these four refused to act in the matter,—plainly on the ground that the law was an unauthorized effort to require the judges to perform work which was not judicial. In Connecticut, the judges sate as commissioners [28] and made findings, one of which was afterwards, as will appear, used as a test-case.

In New York, the Circuit Court [29] took the matter into consideration on April 5, 1792, and referred to the Government's being divided into three branches, each distinct and independent; adding:

Neither the Legislative nor the Executive branches can constitutionally assign to the Judicial any duties but such as are properly judicial. . . . The duties assigned to the Circuit Courts, by this Act, are not of that description.

[27] Story's "Statutes of the United States" (2d edition by George Sharswood), Vol. I, p. 224.
[28] "Note to Hayburn case," 2 Dallas, pp. 410-14, or "American State Papers, Misc.," Vol. I, pp. 49-52.
[29] Duane, of Rutgers v. Waddington memory, was one of the three judges sitting.

Nor (so they went on in effect) does the Act seem to contemplate them as such, inasmuch as it subjects the decisions of the courts in the matter to suspension by the Secretary of War and revision by the Legislature. Hence, the Act can only be considered as appointing commissioners for the purpose, by official instead of personal description, and we think ourselves entitled to accept or decline. We will act, adjourning the court as usual from day to day, but proceeding regularly as commissioners between the adjournments to execute the business of the. Act. A copy of their minutes, setting forth these views, was sent on April 10th to the President, with a request that he would communicate them to Congress.[30]

In North Carolina, the same course was followed, to some extent; but the judges did not think they could act as commissioners. They also sent a letter, dated June 8, 1792, to the President, in which they wrote in part:

We never can find ourselves in a more painful situation than to be obliged to object to the execution of any [Act of the Legislature, but we cannot think the Courts authorized in exercising] power not in its nature judicial, or, if judicial, not provided for upon the terms the Constitution requires. . . . These, Sir, are our reasons for being of opinion . . . that this Circuit Court cannot be justified in the execution of that part of the act, which

---

[30] "Note to Hayburn's case," 2 Dallas, pp. 410-414. Max Farrand's "The First Hayburn Case," in *Amer. Histor. Rev.*, Vol. XII, pp. 281-285.

requires it to examine and report an opinion [on Pension cases].[31]

It was, however, in the Circuit Court for the District of Pennsylvania, where James Wilson presided and had beside him Blair, J. and Peters, District Judge, that the issue came most squarely to a head. It is hard to see how there can be a doubt that, even in the lawyers' sense, they held the Act unconstitutional. The record of their docket tells us baldly that the petition of one Hayburn to be placed upon the list of Pensioners came up before them on April 11, and that when the petition was read, they entered a decree that "after due deliberation thereupon had, it is considered by the Court that the same be not proceeded upon"; but it will shortly be shown that all the extant evidence indicates that the unconstitutionality of the law was their reason, and that it was so announced from the bench. Written statements of the Court itself seem to show the same thing.[32]

In this Circuit also, the Judges addressed a letter (April 18) to the President, in which they wrote that to him it belonged to see the laws faithfully executed, and that therefore they thought it their duty to lay before him

the sentiments which, on a late painful occasion, governed us, with regard to an act passed by the legislature

[31] *Ibid.*

[32] Prof. Farrand suggests to call this "The First Hayburn Case," in order to distinguish it from the case in 2 Dallas, p. 409. To Prof. Farrand's article, already cited, are due nearly all the statements in the text.

of the Union. . . . We have been unanimously of opinion, that, under this Act, the Circuit Court for the District of Pennsylvania could not proceed [1. Because the business assigned to us is not judicial: 2. Because (if we had acted) our judgments might have been revised by the Legislative and Executive Departments]. Such revision and control, we deemed radically inconsistent with the independence of that judicial power which is vested in the courts. . . . These, Sir, are the reasons of our conduct. Be assured that, though it became necessary, it was far from being pleasant. To be obliged to act contrary, either to the obvious directions of Congress, or to a constitutional principle, in our judgment, equally obvious, excited feelings in us which we hope never to experience again.[33]

Almost immediately after the Court's refusal to go on with the case, Hayburn presented (April 13) a memorial to the House of Representatives, setting forth the action of the Court and asking for relief; and there was some consideration of the matter. Boudinot, a member of the House, made an explanatory statement, saying:

The Court thought the examination of invalids a very extraordinary duty to be imposed on the judges and looked upon the law which imposes that duty as an unconstitutional one, inasmuch as it directs the Secretary of War to state the mistakes of the judges to Congress for their revision; they could not, therefore, accede to a regulation tending to render the Judiciary subject to the

[33] "Note to Hayburn's Case" and Prof. Farrand's article, *ut ante.*

Legislative and Executive powers. . . . This being the first instance in which a court of justice had declared a law of Congress to be unconstitutional, the novelty of the case produced a variety of opinions with respect to the measures to be taken on the occasion.[34]

One of the measures suggested, according to some newspapers, was impeachment, which would hardly have been proposed, unless for some such grievous offense as holding a law of Congress unconstitutional.

The *Aurora* of April 20 wrote:

Never was the word "impeachment" so hackneyed as it has been since the spirited sentence passed by our judges on an unconstitutional law. . . . But when these impeachment mongers are asked how any law is to be declared unconstitutional, they tell us that nothing less than a general convention is adequate to pass sentence on it. . . .

On the other hand, Camden, in the same paper of the 21st, disapproved of the article just quoted, as well as of the decision, and denied that any one in Congress had committed himself to impeachment. To this, Freneau's *National Gazette* of April 16 adds:

A correspondent remarks that the late decision of the Judges of the U. S., declaring an act of the present session of Congress *unconstitutional,* must be matter of high

[34] "Annals of Congress, 2d Congress, 1st session," pp. 556, 557. The quotation in the text seems to be the reporter's summation of what Bondinot said, except the latter part as to the instance being the first in which a court had held a law unconstitutional, etc., which is probably entirely the reporter's own opinion. See also Edward S. Corwin's "Doctrine of Judicial Review," pp. 50, 51.

gratification to every republican and friend of liberty. . . . It affords a just hope that . . . any existing law of Congress, which may be supposed to trench upon the constitutional rights of individuals or of States, will, at convenient seasons, undergo a revision; particularly that for establishing a National Bank.

And the same paper of the 23rd contains an article noticing "Camden's" letter in the *Aurora* (quoted above), and saying:

We deny "Camden's" assertion; and assert that the word "impeachment" was several times mentioned in the House of Representatives, although no motion was made on the subject.

And again on May 10, the same *Gazette* spoke of "the decision of the judges against the constitutionality of an act in which the Executive had concurred with the legislative department."

With all this evidence, it is a very moderate claim [35] to make that "there would seem to be no reasonable doubt that on April 11 James Wilson, John Blair and Richard Peters declared the Invalid Pension Act of 1792 unconstitutional." The docket does not, it is true, show this specifically, but on ultratechnical grounds it is hard to see what else can have been the ground for a refusal to proceed with the case. It was plainly no mere temporary postponement, and the evidence from all other sources, in the House of

[35] This is Prof. Farrand's claim in "The First Hayburn Case," *Amer. Histor. Rev.*, Vol. XII, pp. 281-285.

Representatives and out of it, shows conclusively that unconstitutionality was the ground of the decision. The First Hayburn Case was then the earliest instance in which a Federal Court held an act of Congress void.

Attorney-General Randolph moved later in the Supreme Court for a mandamus to the Circuit Court for the District of Pennsylvania to proceed with the petition of Hayburn, but no decision was ever rendered, because Congress, in effect, gave up the question and passed a law for the relief of pensioners in another way.[36]

But this extensively considered question did not end even here. Doubts were entertained as to the validity of the findings of the members of the Circuit Courts, who had sate as commissioners, and section 3 of the Act of 1793 directed a test-case to be brought to raise this point. The Circuit Court in Connecticut had so acted and made a finding in favor of one Todd, and this had been paid. A suit was now brought to recover it, but it is not certain what was the basis of the decree to refund, which was entered against the defendant. Our knowledge of the case depends on a note made by Taney, filed in 1851 by his orders; and he thought that the case ruled that the first pension act conferred power, which was not judicial, and was therefore unconstitutional; but it seems that more modern students are probably right, and that the real reason for the

[36] Hayburn's Case, 2 Dallas, 409. Act of 28 February, 1793, Story's "Statutes of the U. S." (2d Edition, by Geo. Sharswood), Vol. I, p. 304.

decision was that the sitting of the judges as commissioners was held to be unauthorized under the act.[37]

It is not without interest to find that, in the growth and establishment of Judicial Power in America, some views were early held which seem to us to-day very strange. Principles are rarely, or never, brought forth in full panoply of armor at their first appearance, but grow slowly by the retention of what is desirable and the elimination of matters perhaps earnestly contested for by some, but which the more sober judgment of others rules out as impossible, or undesirable.

In 1793, at the time when Genet was making us so much trouble, President Washington, by the advice of his Cabinet, asked the Justices of the Supreme Court a series of questions in relation to our differences with France concerning the provisions of the treaties with her, but the Supreme Court ended forever this attempted perversion of Judicial Power, by replying that "they deemed it improper to enter the field of politics by declaring their opinions on questions not growing out of some case actually before them.[38]

In 1795, the general question arose again in the Circuit Court of Pennsylvania, in Van Horne's Lessee v. Dorrance.[39] The case concerned the well-known

[37] U. S. v. Yale Todd in "Note" to U. S. v. Ferreira, 13 Howard, 52. Farrand's "First Hayburn Case," *Amer. Histor. Rev.*, Vol. XII, pp. 281-285. Thayer's "Cases in Constitutional Law," Vol. I, p. 105 n.

[38] Marshall's "Washington," Vol. V, pp. 433, 441, cited in Simeon E. Baldwin's "The American Judiciary," pp. 33, 34, and in Corwin's "Doctrine of Judicial Review," pp. 50, 51.

[39] 2 Dallas, 304.

dispute between Pennsylvania and Connecticut in regard to certain lands, and the defendant relied on the Quieting and Confirming Act of the former State. Paterson, J.,—whose probable knowledge of Holmes v. Walton and whose connection with the New Jersey Plan in the Convention have been shown,[40]—held the act in question to be in violation of the Federal Constitution, on the ground that it was *ex post facto* and impaired the obligation of a contract, and directed a verdict for the plaintiff. He said:

I take it to be a clear position that if a legislative act oppugns a constitutional principle, the former must give way, and be rejected on the score of repugnance. I hold it to be a position equally clear and sound that, in such a case, it will be the duty of the Court to adhere to the Constitution, and to declare the act null and void. The Constitution is . . . a rule and commission by which both Legislators and Judges are to proceed. . . . It says to the legislators, thus far ye shall go and no further.

A foot-note adds that a writ of error had been taken and was pending in the Supreme Court, but apparently it never came to argument. In U. S. v. Villato,[41] also, in 1797, a Pennsylvania statute concerning naturalization was held void by the Circuit Court, as being in violation of the existing State Constitution.

During the next year after Van Horne v. Dorrance, the question of the Judicial Power reached the Su-

[40] See *ante,* pp. 134, 135.
[41] 2 Dallas, 370.

preme Court for the first time, and in the following
four years there were two other such cases,—making
four in all by 1800, if U. S. v. Yale Todd be included.
In no one of these was there a decision of the point;
but in all language was used which shows how the doctrine was spreading and being accepted by the bench;
evidence will be found, too, that the bar as well was
coming to be saturated with the same belief, and was
beginning to use the new weapon in their pleadings,
and in general, as a means of protecting their clients.

The first case was Hylton v. The United States [42]
in the Circuit Court for Virginia, which was a suit
against Hylton for his neglect to return one hundred
and twenty-five carriages for taxation under the Act
of June 5, 1794. A case stated was filed, in which
it was agreed that Hylton had refused to return the
carriages, "alledging that the said law was unconstitutional and void," and judgment had been entered
against Hylton. He then took a writ of error to this
judgment, and the case was argued by most eminent
counsel: Lee, Attorney-General, and Alexander Hamilton, for the United States, and Campbell, of Virginia,
and Jared Ingersoll, Attorney-General of Pennsylvania, for Hylton. The decision turned on the point
whether or not the tax was a direct one under the
Constitution, and therefore required to be laid according to the rule of apportionment. The Judges were
all of opinion that it was not a direct tax, and was
therefore constitutionally laid, but Paterson wrote:
"If it be a direct tax, it is unconstitutional," while

[42] 3 Dallas, 171.

Chase did not think it a direct tax, and hence regarded it as

> unnecessary, at this time, for me to determine whether this court *constitutionally* possesses the power to declare an Act of Congress *void*, on the ground of its being made contrary to, and in violation of the Constitution, but if the Court have such power, I am free to declare, that I will never exercise it, but in a very clear case.

Hamilton was paid a fee by spcial appropriation of Congress, "for arguing the cause before the Supreme Court in February term, 1796, respecting the constitutionality of the act imposing duties on carriages." [43] Nor should it go unnoted that the point of constitutionality was here again evidently used by counsel: for it cannot be doubted that professional advice led to the recital in the case stated that Hylton had declined to return the carriages for taxation, on the ground that the tax violated the Constitution, and was void.

In 1798 the question of the Court's powers came up once more in the Supreme Court, in Calder *v.* Bull.[44] The case depended on a statute of Connecticut, of 1795, which had set aside a decree of their Probate Court disapproving a certain will, and had granted a new hearing, under which the same will had been approved. Counsel for the plaintiff in error

[43] Speech of Dana on the repeal of the Judiciary Act in 1802, "Annals of Congress, 7th Congress, 1st session," 920-925. Dana was maintaining the power of the Courts and using this fact in the connection. He said, "the principle . . . has been settled for years." Edwin S. Corwin's "Doctrine of Judicial Review," pp. 50, 51.

[44] 3 Dallas, 386.

(against the will admitted at the second hearing), contended "that any law of the Federal Government, or of any of the State Governments, contrary to the *Constitution of the United States, is void;* and that this court possess the power to declare *such* law *void.*" But Chase, J. wrote in evident reply to this:

Without giving an opinion, at this time, whether this court has jurisdiction to decide that any law made by Congress, contrary to the Constitution of the *United States,* is void; I am fully satisfied that this court has no *jurisdiction* to determine that any law of any State *Legislature,* contrary to the Constitution of such *state,* is void.

This was in substance, it seems, the opinion of the Court in general; but Iredell was so clear on certain points that he must be quoted, and it is to be regretted that Judges have not generally remembered what he said. Perhaps, had they done so, and thus confined themselves to reasonable and fixed grounds, there would not to-day be such a hue-and-cry against their real powers. He expressed himself as of opinion that, if a Government of the three Departments was established by a Constitution, which imposed no limits on the legislative power, whatever the Legislature might choose to enact would be lawfully enacted, and the Judiciary could never interpose to declare it void. And then he went on:

It is true, that some speculative jurists have held, that a legislative act against natural justice must, in itself, be void; but I cannot think that, under such a government,

any court of Justice would possess a power to declare it
so. . . . In order, therefore, to guard against so great
an evil, it has been the policy of all the *American* states,
which have, individually, framed their state constitutions
since the revolution, and of the people of the *United
States,* when they framed the Federal Constitution, to
define with precision the objects of the legislative power,
and to restrain its exercise within marked and settled
boundaries. If any Act of Congress, or of the Legislature of a state, violates those constitutional principles, it
is unquestionably void; though I admit, that as the authority to declare it void is of a delicate and awful nature,
the court will never resort to that authority, but in a
clear and urgent case. If, on the other hand, the Legislature of the Union, or the Legislature of any member
of the Union, shall pass a law, within the general scope
of their constitutional power, the Court cannot pronounce it to be void, merely because it is, in their judgment, contrary to the principles of natural justice. The
ideas of natural justice are regulated by no fixed standard.

Once more, in the last year of the century, the
question was under consideration in the Supreme
Court, but again failed to call for an actual decision.
Cooper *v.* Telfair [45] was a suit by Cooper of Jamaica
against Telfair of Georgia, on a bond executed by the
latter in 1774. Telfair pleaded the Act of Georgia of
1782 for the confiscation of the property of those
guilty of treason,—which expressly named Cooper,—
and that by a later law of Georgia, of 1787, the amount

[45] 4 Dallas, 14.

of the bond had been forfeited to the State. To this Cooper replied,—and again here we may safely assume that we have an instance of the astuteness of counsel,—that he had never been tried and convicted or attainted of treason, and that by the Georgia Constitution of 1777, the Legislative, Executive, and Judiciary were directed to be kept separate and distinct, so that neither should exercise the power belonging to the other. The Court below held this reply insufficient, and that the plea, setting up the confiscation, was a full defense, and entered judgment for the defendant on the demurrer. The plaintiff then took a writ of error, and set up that the judgment held that the Legislature had cognizance of the alleged treason and could legally convict him.

Upon the argument in the Supreme Court, E. Tilghman maintained:

If the law is contrary to the Constitution, the law is void; and the judiciary authority, either of the state, or of the *United States,* may pronounce it to be so. 2 Dallas, 308, 410. 3 Dallas, 383.[46] The law is contrary to the constitution, inasmuch as it is an exercise of the judicial power by the legislative authority, in opposition to an express prohibition of such a union of jurisdiction.

Defendant's counsel, Ingersoll and Dallas, "conceded that, if the law plainly and obviously violates the Constitution of Georgia, it is void," but contended that it did not.

The judgment below was affirmed, Cushing saying

[46] The reference to 3 Dallas is a mis-citation.

that, although in his opinion they had "the same power that a Court of the state of Georgia would possess, to declare the law void, I do not think the occasion would warrant an exercise of the power"; while Chase wrote of an unconstitutional law being void:

Yet, it still remains a question, where the power resides to declare it void. It is, indeed, a general opinion, it is expressly admitted by all this bar, and some of the Judges have, individually, in the Circuit Courts, decided, that the Supreme Court can declare an Act of Congress to be unconstitutional, and therefore, invalid; but there is no adjudication of the Supreme Court itself upon the point.

True though these last words were, yet all the gathering forces and all the signs of the times foretold plainly enough that such a decision of the highest court was near to hand; and before three years of the new century had gone by, Marbury *v*. Madison arose, and Marshall received for his opinion perhaps more praise than was due, but still it was written with all the clear reasoning of the great Chief Justice, and has never since been departed from among us.

Before proceeding to it, however, it will be well to recall to the reader that (as others have already noticed) the Legislative Department had passed at least one law directing a test case to be brought before the Judiciary, in order to ascertain the opinion of the highest court on the constitutionality of a law. This had been done as to the controverted Pension Law of 1792, and the validity of decrees made by the judges sitting as commissioners after their refusal to hear the cases as a court.[47] Surely, for the Legislature to appeal to the Judiciary for its opinion on the constitutionality of a law, which the Legislature has itself enacted, is a striking example of the recognition of the Judicial Power.

In one other instance the Legislative Department discussed the general problem, and by an enormous preponderance of voices added its evidence to the proof that the Judiciary did rightfully possess the power it was now claiming all over the country. In 1802, upon the repeal by the triumphant Republicans of the Judiciary Bill, which they feared would saddle them for many years with the Federal Judges appointed in such unbecoming haste in the last days of John Adams's presidency, the question was discussed by numbers of Senators and Representatives whether or not such a law would be unconstitutional and could be held void by the Judiciary. The debate is far too long and scattering to be gone into here, but Mason of Massachusetts; Tracy, Dana, and Griswold of Connecticut; Gouverneur Morris of New York (a member of the Convention of 1787); Ross and Hemphill of Pennsylvania; Bayard of Delaware; Smith of Vermont; John Rutledge of South Carolina (a member of the Convention of 1787); Dennis of Maryland, and Henderson and Stanley of North Carolina, all spoke of the doctrine with approval, while only Stevens T. Mason of Virginia, Stone of North Carolina, and Brecken-

[47] *Ante,* p. 184.

ridge of Kentucky seem to have been on the other side.[48]

To indicate how fully the Judicial Power was already accepted, it may be stated that Hemphill spoke in this early debate of its denial as "a doctrine new and dangerous"; while Henderson said that, if Congress can repeal the Judiciary Act, the Judiciary are in control of the Legislature, and

Whatever the Legislature declares to be law must be obeyed. The constitutional check which the judges were to be on the Legislature is completely done away. They may pass *ex post facto* laws, bills of attainder. . . . The monstrous and unheard of doctrine which has been lately advanced, that the judges have not the right of declaring unconstitutional laws void, will be put into practice by the adoption of this measure [*i. e.,* by the repeal of the Judiciary Act].

[48] For Henderson and Stanley, *see* Benton's "Abridgment," Vol. II, pp. 599, and 601. For the rest see "Review of Vol. XII of Sergeant and Rawle's (Penna.) Reports," and especially of Judge Gibson's denial of the judicial power in Eakin *v.* Raub reported in that volume, in *Amer. Quar. Review,* Vol. II, pp. 186-214. This "Review" was said by Chas. J. Ingersoll in his speech in the Pennsylvania Constitutional Convention of 1838 upon the repeal of bank charters to be by Judge Hopkinson, but I am unable to demonstrate that such was the case. Judge Hopkinson's grandson, Edward Hopkinson, Esq., of the Philadelphia bar, tells me that he knows nothing in regard to whether the review was written by his grandfather or not. It at least certainly came from an able pen. The fact must be borne in mind that partisanship entered strongly into the debate. I used these details in my article "Some Recent Attacks on the American Doctrine of Judicial Power" in *Amer. Law Rev.* (1906), Vol. XL, pp. 641-670: see especially, p. 652. I have not verified the list of names of the author of the "Review," but the words quoted in the text from Henderson are taken by myself from Benton's "Abridgment."

Here was,—by the very early days of the nineteenth century and within fifteen years from the date when the Constitution went into effect,—an overwhelming mass of decision and opinion asserting the power of the Judiciary in regard to unconstitutional laws, and there was extremely little contrary opinion,—only some scattering views of individuals and a few contests made in the Legislatures, whose possible powers were so greatly shorn by the rapidly growing principle.

And the decisions made covered the whole field. They were not at all confined to State laws violating the Constitution of the State or the Federal powers, but laws passed by Congress without authority under the Federal Constitution had equally been held in several instances to be subject to the same sifting process in the Courts. The belief in this latter branch of the subject, as well as in the voidness of unauthorized State laws, was well-nigh universal, and rapidly coming to be an established principle,—a new chapter of the law, well known to lawyers, and used by them in the study and preparation of their cases.

The only difference still existing in regard to unauthorized laws of the Federal Government and of the States, was that there had as yet been no decision in the former class of cases, in the highest Court of the Union,—as there had been in a number of instances in the Supreme Courts of the States. The Federal decisions were all as yet in the lower Courts, but this difference was swept away as early as 1803 by Marbury *v.* Madison. The indications had been overwhelming that such would be the outcome, as the principle kept spreading steadily: but the final step came perhaps sooner than is often the case in the evolution of governmental principles.

Marbury *v*. Madison grew out of a partisan quarrel. When the Federalists were defeated in the election of 1800 and Jefferson was elected to the Presidency, the defeated party aimed to fill up all the offices with their adherents, and this was perhaps especially the case as to judicial positions, the incumbents of which could not at once be dismissed by the incoming Republicans. Down to the very end of his term, John Adams was making appointments to vacant and new offices, and a number of the commissions had not yet been actually delivered when he went out of office. Some such commissions appointing Justices of the Peace for the District of Columbia were found in the Secretary of State's Office by Madison, the incoming Secretary. They were not delivered by him.

William Marbury and three others, named as Justices of the Peace in such undelivered commissions, thereupon applied in December, 1801, to the Supreme Court of the United States for a writ of *mandamus* to command Madison to deliver their commissions to them. They were represented by Charles Lee, Attorney-General under the late administration; their claim being that, as the nominations had been made by the President and approved by the Senate, and commissions then made out and duly recorded in the State Department, their appointment to a judicial office was complete, and the commissions must be delivered. The delivery, it was maintained, was a mere ministerial act, to which the Secretary of State could be compelled by judicial process.

No one appeared or argued the case on behalf of the defense, as the administration looked upon the proceeding as entirely unauthorized, and declined to recognize it in any way. And when (in accordance with the practice in cases of *mandamus*) a rule on the defendant to show cause why the writ should not issue, was granted, Madison took no notice of it whatever.

At a later term, on final hearing, the case was argued by Lee on behalf of the plaintiff alone, and all the main contentions of the plaintiff were sustained by the Chief Justice in an argument of no little length; but the opinion did not stop here. It went on to show that the Supreme Court had no jurisdiction at all in the case, owing to a flaw in the method adopted to get at the result desired. It was true that the law of Congress establishing the Courts authorized the Supreme Court

to issue writs of mandamus, in cases warranted by the principles and usages of law, to any . . . persons holding office, under the authority of the United States.

But was this statute authorized under the terms of the Constitution, which provided that

The Supreme Court shall have original jurisdiction in all cases affecting ambassadors, other public ministers and consuls, and those in which a state shall be a party. In all other cases, the supreme court shall have appellate jurisdiction.

Could Congress confer original jurisdiction ön the Supreme Court in a case of *mandamus,* or in any case, except those enumerated by the Constitution?

This was the great constitutional question which Marshall discussed,—at no great length,—and reached the conclusion that Congress could not do so, that the statute conferring original jurisdiction in such case was unconstitutional and void. The rule for a *mandamus* was therefore discharged and, so far as is known, no further proceedings were taken in the matter, despite the fact that Marshall had gone so far out of his way, into the regions of *obiter dicta,*[49] to indicate the proper legal method of raising the question that the plaintiffs sought to have determined.

Marshall's argument on the constitutional point has been the subject of extravagant praise from some, Kent [50] speaking of it as "approaching to the precision and certainty of a mathematical demonstration," but others have been less laudatory. The truth is that not much new could then be said upon the subject, for the ground had often been covered by others. The absolute necessity of the Judiciary's having the power to hold laws unconstitutional, unless our written Constitutions were to be waste paper and the limitations to fail utterly, was palpable, but perhaps a strong technical argument could have been made that the limitations were directory to the legislators, and merely binding on their consciences,—as are undoubtedly

[49] Of course, the Republicans charged him with partisanship, and with apparent reason, for, when a court once decides that it has no jurisdiction, it has no further function.

[50] "Commentaries," Vol. I, p. 453.

many of the very similar commands contained in Constitutions. It will be best to let the opinion speak for
itself, and the reader will certainly find in it the clear
and logical method of the great Chief Justice, whatever else may be said.

The Constitution, he wrote, extends the judicial
power of the United States to all cases arising under
the Constitution, and then he asked whether it could
be the intention that in such cases the Constitution
should not be looked into,—that a case arising under
the Constitution shall be decided without examining
the instrument under which it arises? "This is too
extravagant to be maintained." The oath required
of the Judges was also borne upon, as well as the
immorality of imposing it on them, "if they were to
be used as the instruments, and the knowing instruments, for violating what they swear to support."
But the following seems to be the main portion of his
proof of "the principle, supposed to be essential to
all written constitutions, that a law repugnant to the
constitution is void; and that *courts,* as well as other
departments, are bound by the instrument":

The question, whether an act, repugnant to the constitution, can become the law of the land, is a question
deeply interesting to the United States; but, happily, not
of an intricacy proportioned to its interest. It seems
only necessary to recognize certain principles, supposed
to have been long and well established, to decide it.

That the people have an original right to establish, for
their future government, such principles as, in their opinion, shall most conduce to their own happiness is the

basis on which the whole American fabric has been erected. The exercise of this original right is a very great exertion; nor can it, nor ought it, to be frequently repeated. The principles, therefore, so established, are deemed fundamental. And as the authority from which they proceed is supreme, and can seldom act, they are designed to be permanent.

This original and supreme will organizes the government, and assigns to different departments their respective powers. It may either stop here, or establish certain limits not to be transcended by those departments.

The government of the United States is of the latter description. The powers of the legislature are defined and limited; and that those limits may not be mistaken, or forgotten, the constitution is written. To what purpose are powers limited, and to what purpose is that limitation committed to writing, if these limits may, at any time, be passed by those intended to be restrained? The distinction between a government with limited and unlimited powers is abolished, if those limits do not confine the persons on whom they are imposed, and if acts prohibited and acts allowed, are of equal obligation. It is a proposition too plain to be contested, that the constitution controls any legislative act repugnant to it; or, that the legislature may alter the constitution by an ordinary act.

Between these alternatives there is no middle ground. The constitution is either a superior paramount law, unchangeable by ordinary means, or it is on a level with ordinary legislative acts, and, like other acts, is alterable when the legislature shall please to alter it.

If the former part of the alternative be true, then a legislative act contrary to the constitution is not law: if the latter part be true, then written constitutions are absurd attempts, on the part of the people, to limit a power in its own nature illimitable.

Certainly all those who have framed written constitutions contemplate them as forming the fundamental and paramount law of the nation, and, consequently, the theory of every such government must be, that an act of the legislature, repugnant to the constitution, is void.

This theory is essentially attached to a written constitution, and, is consequently, to be considered, by this court, as one of the fundamental principles of our society.

With this decision in the highest court of the country, the power in question became, in fact, settled. That Marbury v. Madison was a potent factor in the history of the matter cannot be doubted; but this was, I think, owing to the elevated platform from which Marshall spoke, and to the fact that the decision stood out as the culmination of a long and gradual growth, rather than to any very remarkable power of argument contained in the opinion.

Since the decision of Holmes v. Walton in 1780, the power of the Judiciary has been exercised in our country in hosts upon hosts of cases. Many thousand State laws have, beyond doubt, been held invalid in the States themselves, because of violating either the Constitution of the State in question or that of the United States. By 1912 as many as 223 State laws and 23 municipal ordinances had been held void by the Supreme Court of the United States, on the ground that they conflicted with the Federal Constitution, and 33 laws of Congress had met the same fate, because they were held not to be authorized under that instrument.[51]   These cases, too, were scattered over the whole period in question, though by far the greater number of those in relation to laws of the United States occurred after 1830, and they were carried into effect, in the vast majority of instances, without dispute.

In the very early days of the doctrine, Trevett *v.* Weeden was violently denounced, and the Judges not reëlected; Rutgers *v.* Waddington was equally denounced by a section of the public; Bayard *v.* Singleton was a subject of earnest dispute, and others of the earliest cases did not go without protest, but in general the exercise of the Judicial Power was readily accepted or even welcomed.

Of course, there continued to be for a number of years sporadic expressions of opinion to the contrary. Thus, in Pennsylvania in 1808, in Emerick *v.* Harris,[52] it was strenuously argued before the Supreme Court of the State, by very eminent counsel, that the Judiciary did not possess the power in question, and the Court went into an argument of some length to prove the existence of such power.   Again, as late as 1843 the same argument was once more made in Pennsylvania, in Commonwealth *v.* Mann.[53]   The denial of

[51] B. F. Moore's "The Supreme Court and Unconstitutional Legislation" (Columbia College Studies, Vol. 54, No. 2), Chapter III.   The author's tables include decisions rendered in 1911.
[52] I Binney, p. 416.
[53] 5 Watts and Sergeant, p. 503.

the power in the same State by Judge Gibson,—except so far as related to State laws violating the Federal Constitution,—in his dissent in Eakin *v.* Raub[54] in 1825, is well known, but this very able Pennsylvania judge recalled this opinion in 1845 in Menges v. Wertman.[55] Like cases probably exist in other States.

In the earlier years of the nineteenth century, too, there were a few wide-extended and bitter contests, more or less of a political nature, over the question in several of our States; Ohio, Georgia, Kentucky, South Carolina,[56] and perhaps other States, were the scenes of such struggles. But in all these instances, despite the fire and fury which accompanied them, not only did the particular decision stand, but the doctrine was enforced in other cases, and was ere long generally recognized to be established law. In all our States, as well as in the sphere covered by the United States, the Power of the Judiciary came in time to be not only accepted but to be appealed to,—much as the writ of *habeas corpus* is appealed to,—as a palladium of our liberties. The contests all fell by the wayside, as incidents of little moment, while the public accepted more

[54] 12 Sergeant and Rawle, p. 330.

[55] I Penna. State Reports, p. 218. See also Norris *v.* Clymer, 2 *ibid.,* p. 281.

[56] Some account of these contests will be found in Baldwin's "American Judiciary," pp. 111-16. See also J. B. Thayer's "American Doctrine," etc., *Harvard Law Review,* Vol. VII, p. 8, etc., and for the contest in Ohio, see *Western Law Monthly* (June, 1863), Vol. V, p. 4, etc. For the contest in South Carolina, I can give no certain reference, but am satisfied that in the correspondence of Charles Jared Ingersoll (M. C. 1813-15) I saw a letter (dated between 1818 and 1825?) from a friend in South Carolina who had been in Congress with him, referring to the dispute there.

and more widely the view that a statute in violation of either the State or the Federal Constitution is void, and that it is the function of the Judiciary so to decide in any law case depending before them. The unanimity was long astonishing.

For this very reason, the outburst of recent years against our well-established doctrine is most remarkable. Launched, as it seems, by a few Progressives, it was beyond doubt the expression of some latent popular feeling; for it has certainly gained strength, and no one can now tell what the outcome may be. There is a wide-spread feeling in the body politic that constitutional limitations are a mere hindrance, and that the majority voice of the people of this vast country should have undisputed sway in all things, despite the fact that the limitations were, of course, written into the Constitution for the express purpose of curbing the brute majority, and in order to protect the rights of a minority. But this historic truth may well in the end go for nought, in a time when our country is engaged in such a furious war as that of to-day. A body composed of a few fallible men sitting as a Court, and perhaps holding unconstitutional and void some vital element in the system of taxation or other essential branch of the administration of a great Empire, might be very inconvenient, if not even destructive, in a time such as that we live in.

But the war of to-day will not last forever, nor was the propaganda started with it in view. Probably, the real motive, whether conscious or unconscious, of these gentlemen was that they might be able to enact all sorts of socialistic legislation, to try raw experiments which a few of their number might dream out as a sure-cure for the little rubs which, under the existing system, do undoubtedly arise.

Many of our public men, and even of our most known leaders, have for a number of years shown the tendency, to which reference has been already made, to be highly impatient under the restrictions of constitutional or legal limitations. These restrictions stand, in their view, for mere impediments to be gotten rid of, in order that they may work out with a free hand any pet theory of the moment. And this tendency is of older date than some think. Andrew Jackson was probably the first of our Executives to show it; and he was ever convinced that his pet beliefs were entitled to supreme sway. His successors for some years had far less of the tendency; but in modern days it has grown again with giant strides, and now the furious war of the Germans has added an enormous impetus.

That the tendency in question is most serious and likely to have far-reaching consequences in many ways is certain; but in regard to the question of Judicial Power, its dangers seem more menacing and perhaps more imminent than in other directions. A highly progressive member from a new Western State has already proposed in the Senate to curb the Judicial Power by a statute providing in effect for the removal of any Federal Judge, by the mere passage of a Congressional resolution calling upon the President to nominate his successor. Other proposals in the same general direction have also been made, and soon after the Civil War some politicians, who were displeased at certain decisions of the Supreme Court, wanted to require two-thirds of the Court, in order to hold an act of Congress void, and to authorize the removal of Judges upon legislative address, as well as to appoint a special tribunal to decide constitutional questions. But none of these plans has as yet had any success.[57]

We have lived so long under the old system, and our legislatures had come to depend upon it so generally, that to oust the historical Judicial Power root and branch, even though it were done gradually, would probably land us in chaos. It would take many, many years for the hosts of American law-makers to acquire the habit of thinking carefully for themselves of questions of constitutional right,—even assuming that they could ever do so,—and our many statute-books would certainly be loaded down with all sorts of raw statutes, not half thought out and sure to be very unjust to individuals.

But the future must take care of itself, and in some way our country may yet reach a safe anchorage and a system as good as,—or better than,—that which we have known in our day by a happy inheritance from our ancestors. The raw methods and ideas of the Progressives will in this event hardly continue to be

[57] "Congressional Record, 62d Cong., First Sess.," p. 3359. *Ibid.*, "63d Cong., First Sess., H. J. Res," 114. *Ibid.*, 63d Cong., First Sess., p. 1052. I take these references from William S. Carpenter's "Judicial Tenure in the United States" (Yale University Press, 1918), pp. 140-42.

those controlling our public affairs, even if this faction should succeed in breaking down much that we inherited, and mortising into our system some of their socialistic and paternal-government principles,—all, curiously enough, derived in the main from the system prevailing in the German Empire under the benign rule of Bismarck and the Hohenzollerns, which system we and other nations are to-day struggling with our utmost power to break down, so as to render the world "safe for Democracy."

CHAPTER X

THE DEGREE OF CONCLUSIVENESS ATTACHING TO JUDI-
CIAL DECISIONS. EARLY BELIEFS ON THE SUBJECT.
THE FUTURE.

THERE remains one other very important subject in
relation to Judicial Power, of which it is my intention
to treat in this book,—though by no means exhaust-
ively. That would lead us far afield and touch upon
many instances reeking with partisanship, and hence
would be very likely to be misleading. Perhaps the
point I refer to may be indicated by the question: Is
the American Doctrine properly described as of Judicial Power, or of Judicial Supremacy?

One of the very recent books upon the subject is
even named "The American Doctrine of Judicial
Supremacy," and there can be no shadow of doubt but
that among the public in general, as well as by many
students, the view is absolutely accepted that opinions
of the Judiciary bind and conclude the President, Congress, and all the rest of the world. When the Courts
have decided, for instance, that Congress possesses,
or does not possess, a certain power under the clause
to regulate commerce among the States, or that the
President can be deprived of his unlimited constitutional power of appointment to new offices, by a Con-

gressional statute making appropriations for certain work "to be done under the supervision of" So-and-So, there is, according to this view, no question but that the President must nominate this particular person. So Johnson's right to refuse to obey laws, which in his opinion impaired his constitutional right to command the army, or his right of removal from office, is absolutely denied by these gentlemen.

They say that it is the "peculiar function" of the Judiciary to interpret the Constitution, and there is undoubtedly a sense in which these words are true; but such general phrases are likely to be very misleading, and often result in grave error when applied to all circumstances. One well-known author, arguing that decisions of the Courts are conclusive on the other departments, writes that

> The authority of a decision . . . comes from the fact that it is an exercise of the judicial power of the government in a case for the disposal of which this judicial power has been properly invoked.[1]

But why should such a judicial decision carry any more weight, in regard to the underlying general principle involved, than an opposite and perhaps earlier conclusion of Congress, or of the President, rendered in a like case for which its, or his, power has been properly invoked? The special controversy of the individuals concerned is, of course, settled and ended by the judicial decision; but why should this be car-

[1] "The American Judiciary," by Simeon E. Baldwin, pp. 57, 58.

ried to the extent of holding that the opinion of the Court as to the meaning of the Constitution is to be accepted as a finality?

It can hardly be questioned,—and later pages will demonstrate this fact,—that in all our history, down at least to comparatively recent years (and the same view is still held by not a few), the doctrine was by no means admitted that judicial decisions interpreting the Constitution conclude the other great departments of government in regard to the meaning of that instrument,—especially when the extent of the powers of the department in question is concerned. They never are heard, and probably have not even the poor right to be heard, upon the argument of the litigation in question. How, then, has it come to be thought, in the teeth of the early beliefs and of a long line of precedents, that they are concluded?

The growth of this view has been a gradual one, and is evidently the result of the nature and method of the Judiciary's functions. The Judiciary have undoubtedly the right, and it is their peculiar function, to interpret the Constitution in law-suits before them, in so far as relates to the rights of all parties litigant. The very purpose of their existence is to settle disputes, and prevent violence and private feuds between citizens. Their decisions, too, become quickly "precedents" of practically binding force, so far as relates to the rights of all citizens, and this additional force accorded to their interpretations ever tends to spread, have wider influence and to be accepted by all the world, much as if their interpretation were a dictionary clause written into the Constitution or statute.

Nor is even this all that gives strength to the opinions of the Courts. From their very nature and method, they have the most persuasive influence on all the world. The earnest effort to reach an impartial conclusion, the extensive arguments of counsel, in leading cases sure to be men of brilliant intellect and of vast experience, who have ransacked the world in the search for knowledge of the subject from all points of view, and the carefully weighed decisions,—the gist, in important cases, of all the long history of mankind,—properly give to judicial opinions a persuasive weight, which belongs to but few things of human origin. ·

But it does not follow from all this that they bind the other primordial branches of the Government; that they can, for instance, conclude the President as to a question of his power, under the terms of the Constitution, to command the army or to remove from office. The written Constitution has said in most specific words that "the President shall be Commander-in-Chief of the army," and shall have the right to appoint to office, and again (by implication) the right to remove from office. When, then, a question arises as to his right of command under these words, or as to his right to appoint whom he pleases, or to remove at will a hostile or otherwise uncongenial officer, he must decide for himself what is the meaning of these words of the Constitution, precisely as the Courts must do when they are called upon in a suit to enter a decree concerning the rights of litigants under some statute and these or other words of the Constitution. To accept always the opinion of the Judiciary in such cases as to the power of the Executive, or of Congress, would accord to one mere department, among several of equal authority, an absolute control very hostile to the genius of Anglo-Saxon as of popular government.

This question of the right of the different governmental departments to act for themselves within the scope of their authority, as each may understand the constitutional provisions, is not confined to disputes between the Judiciary and some other coördinate branch, but is a general one, and may arise between any two Departments, or between the branches of the Legislature, as well as in other instances. The same general rule ought to obtain in all such cases; and the better opinion and only workable theory seems clearly to be that each Department or agency is free,—in abstract right as well as in actual fact,—to proceed upon its own interpretation of the Constitution and understanding of the circumstances. That they have this power in actual fact and have often exercised it is certainly true, and the distinction is a very shadowy one, which concedes this truth, and yet maintains that theoretically the Department concerned is obliged to follow the expressed opinion of some other Department.

Numbers of instances have occurred in history, in which the general question has arisen. When, for example, the President and Senate have made a Treaty with another Power, which calls for a money-payment by us, the affirmative action of the House of Representatives is undoubtedly essential under our Constitution to the payment of the money concerned. Is the House in such a case obliged in right,—of course, it cannot be actually compelled,—to go on at once and make the necessary appropriation, or has it the constitutional right to consider the merits of the question and even to refuse its assent? Has it any discretion in the matter? At times, the former theory has been strongly asserted, and this view would probably still find supporters; but it seems that the prevailing opinion to-day is to the contrary, and admits that the House has in such a case a complete right to consider the merits of the matter.[2] At the time of the purchase of Alaska,[3] this seems to have been admitted, and it has, I think, been generally admitted since. The same view, moreover, prevails in England.[4]

Again, in England the Legislative Department has always been very determined in resisting control by the other branches, and the privileges of Parliament largely grew up through repeated struggles with the

[2] I do not forget that national faith might in some cases make it very difficult or even impossible for the House justly to refuse its assent, but this is only one element of the problem. The treaty power is a very difficult subject, and especially in recent years some writers have claimed almost unlimited authority under the right to make treaties. But these writers claim too much, and it was certainly a very strange course for the Constitutional Convention to take such infinite trouble to limit the powers of the proposed government, and then by the treaty power to confer the right to do practically anything.

[3] Adams's "Gallatin," p. 161.

[4] Lecky's "England," Vol. I, pp. 154-57. Schouler's "United States," Vol. I, pp. 308, 309, and note. McMaster's "United States," Vol. II, pp. 270-73.

Judiciary and the Executive.[5] The Commons never admitted that the decrees of the Judiciary bound them. On the contrary, there are well-known instances in modern times, in which the popular branch violently denounced such decrees and prevented their enforcement.

These were cases in which there was a clash between some privilege claimed by the Commons, and the ordinary principle that a judicial decree in a suit between parties is final and must be enforced. In one of the cases, for example, the Courts held that there was a private libel contained in the Report of a Committee of the Commons, published by the latter's command, and a judgment was accordingly entered against the public printer; while the Commons, on the other hand, would not permit this judgment to be executed, but asserted their privilege, that it was for them to decide what it was proper to order printed.[6] Otherwise (such was doubtless their view), they could not legislate intelligently and to the best interests of the public.

Here seems to be a strange difference of view and of action between ourselves and the country from which we took our origin. In our supposed "turbulent" democracy, the decrees of the Judiciary, telling the Legislature or the Executive the limits of their

---

[5] See, e.g., Hallam's "Constitutional History of England," Vol. I, pp. 268-75, 302, 303: Vol. II, pp. 43, 440 et seq.: Vol. III, pp. 21 et seq., 27-32, 264 et seq., 271-74, 278.

[6] Stockdale v. Hansard, 9 Ad. and El., i; 11 Ad. and El., 253, 273, 297; Wason v. Walter, L.R. 4 Q.B. 73; Hallam's "Const. Hist.," etc., Vol. III, pp. 271-84; Campbell's "Life of Brougham," Chap. 228 (Ed. Estes & Lauriat, Boston, 1875, pp. 491-93); May's "Constitutional History of England," Vol. I, pp. 423-26.

powers, are apparently to be accepted absolutely, at once, and with docility; while in the limited monarchy, the Parliament, and more especially the Commons, burst out into a fury of turbulence and of excessive passion when the Courts render a decree trenching upon an action of the Commons. How did this difference come about, and what was the origin of the belief in Judicial *Supremacy* held to-day by many in our country?

There were, of course, in the early days of the doctrine all manner of doubts and difficulties, and some curious and interesting opinions were expressed. Thus, Iredell wrote in 1786, in his Letter of an "Elector," rather taking the view that the Judges, should they enforce an unauthorized statute, would, perhaps, be incurring some serious liability. To quote his assertion:

The judges, therefore must take care at their peril, that every act of Assembly they presume to enforce is warranted by the constitution, since if it is not, they act without lawful authority.[7]

On the other hand, the erratic Judge Chase, of the United States Circuit Court, in the very same breath in which he wrote in 1800 that an unconstitutional statute was void, went on[8] to say:

Yet, it still remains a question where the power resides to declare it void. It is, indeed, a general opinion, it is expressly admitted by all this bar, and some of the Judges

[7] Quoted *ante*, p. 112.
[8] Cooper *v.* Telfair, 4 Dallas, 14. See *ante*, pp. 190-192.

have, individually, in the Circuit Courts, decided, that the Supreme Court can declare an act of Congress to be unconstitutional, and, therefore, invalid; but there is no adjudication of the Supreme Court itself upon this point.

Chase's colleague, Cushing, was, on the other hand, already of opinion that they did have the power. This same question had been touched upon, too, in the Pension Cases in 1792, and the partisan *Aurora*,[9] which supported the refusals of the Judges to act under the statute there in question, stated that the opponents of Judicial Power admitted that, according to their view, there was no agency, short of a Constitutional Convention, which could decide a statute unconstitutional.

Here was almost a *reductio ad absurdum,* and here we may doubtless find one of the controlling reasons why the Courts took up the power. As has been said before in these pages, and as thousands have clearly seen, unless they had done so, all the carefully drawn provisions and restrictions of the Constitution would have been futile, and the discretion of Congress have become our only Constitution. The absolute necessity of the case was palpable, and it is not characteristic of a competent people to draw up an elaborate instrument and then fail to find a means to enforce it. Prior pages have shown, too, many other tendencies in our earlier history, which pointed clearly to the conclusion to which our ancestors came upon this point.

At the same time, while some held these doubts in the early days under our present Constitution, there

[9] *Aurora* (Philadelphia), April 20, 1792. See *ante,* p.182.

was no dream on the part of our Courts of claiming what has since come to be called "Judicial Supremacy." When they began to decide, with no little hesitation, that in a law-suit pending before them they could hold a statute unconstitutional and hence refuse to enforce it, they were very careful not to assert even a Judicial Superiority. As it was, they were charged with "dispensing with laws,"[10]—a very unpopular relic of the Stuart kings. Supremacy was not in their dreams, and *equality* was all they claimed,—that, as they were one of the great primordial Departments established by the Constitution, it could not be their duty to accept slavishly and against their clear convictions of the meaning of the instrument, the conclusion of a partisan majority of the legislature that it had power to pass a law, for example, depriving a citizen of his property without a trial by jury. "The obligation of their oaths and the duty of their office" was much borne upon in the anxious opinion in Bayard *v.* Singleton.

In one of the earliest cases, too, one of the judges wrote that he did

not consider the judiciary as the champions of the people or of the constitution, bound to sound the alarm and to excite an opposition to the Legislature. But when the causes of individuals are brought before the judiciary, they are bound to decide.

And if one man claim under an act contrary to the constitution, that is, under what is *no* law (if my former position that the Legislature can not impugn the consti-

[10] In North Carolina, at the time of Bayard *v.* Singleton. See Battle's "Address on the History of the Supreme Court," printed in 103 North Carolina, pp. 445 *et seq.;* 470, 471.

tution, and consequently that an act against it is void, be just) must not a court give judgment against him? [11]

At a much later date, this limited view of their power was still held, and the matter was thus summed up by an able pen (perhaps Judge Hopkinson) in 1827, nearly fifty years after the first decision of the kind was rendered:

We must always bear in mind, that the judiciary do not claim a right directly to annul an Act of the Legislature, by virtue of a superior or superintending power over that department. . . . No such interference with the legislature is pretended—no such superiority over them claimed. But when the judiciary are called upon to execute the illegal act—*to become parties auxiliaries to the usurpation,* they may, not as a superior, but as a *coördinate* branch of the government, refuse their participation in the wrong.[12]

Other citations to this same general effect, from judicial decisions and from writers of authority, could probably be found, but the following only will be quoted. It comes from a "Note" to the case of White *v.* Kendrick[13] in South Carolina in 1805. The unknown author, after speaking of its being plainly the power and duty of courts to declare void all laws contrary to the Constitution, goes on:

[11] Nelson, in Kamper *v.* Hawkins, 2 Virginia Cases, p. 201.
[12] Article already cited from an anonymous writer in *The Amer. Quarterly Review* for 1827, Vol. II, pp. 186, etc., 213. See *ante,* p. 194.
[13] 1 Brevard p. 469.

This right implies no superiority of the judiciary to the legislative power. Each department of the government is the constitutional judge of its own powers; each within its own sphere. The legislative body may enact a law, which they may conceive to be constitutional, but the judiciary may refuse to execute it, if they believe it is not so.

How, then, did the belief in Judicial Supremacy originate? It is curious to find that in 1802 it was threatened by an orator in Congress, as likely to grow out of the very modest claims then making for that branch of government.

To quote Stevens T. Mason when, in 1802, he spoke on the proposed repeal of the Judiciary Act:

They [the judges] may, as gentlemen have told us, hold the constitution in one hand, and the law in the other, and say to the Departments of Government, so far shall you go and no farther. This independence of the Judiciary so much desired, will, I fear, sir, if encouraged or tolerated, soon become something like supremacy.[14]

The earliest approach to a claim of judicial finality known to me is to be found in a statement of Madison's, that at the time of the Alien and Sedition Acts,

the principle was asserted . . . that a sanction given to the Acts by the supreme judicial tribunal of the Union was a bar to any interposition whatever on the part of the States, even in the form of a legislative declaration that the acts in question were unconstitutional.[15]

[14] Benton's "Abridgment," Vol. II, pp. 556, 557.
[15] Paper of 1836 on "Nullification," in "Works," by Congress, 1865, Vol. IV, p. 396; and see pp. 403, 404, 509.

But, whatever partisanship there may have been in this contention, probably the real origin of it, and of the claim in general for Judicial Supremacy, is to be found in the nature of the action of the Judiciary.

One phase of this has already been referred to, but there is another. The vast majority of instances come to that branch for final governmental action. Congress passes a tax-law, the Treasury proceeds to carry it out, and, in case there is a dispute as to the power, the Judiciary is then called upon, and its action in such cases must end the matter, unless some other Department undertakes very unusual methods. Probably the great majority of laws find their final execution in this way at the hands of the Courts,—all the vast mass of legislation relating to contracts, deeds, wills, promissory notes, corporations, and the thousand other matters which concern the usual routine of business affairs and of domestic relations.

In all these cases, the world at large inevitably grows used to looking to the Courts for the settlement of the meaning of statutes and of the Constitution. Their interpretation, so far as each particular case is concerned, is at once accepted. It touches in its immediate effect only the citizen, and there is, hence, no one who can contest it. Their opinion, too, is soon applied in other cases and thus quickly acquires the weight that belongs to precedents in Anglo-Saxon countries. The world soon comes to look upon their interpretation as a part of the statute itself.

It should be remembered, however, that the force

accorded by us to precedents does not by any means essentially and everywhere belong to them. In the Civil Law, generally, the rule is very different; and Sir Henry Maine tells us[16] that in Rome, where the magistrates held office for but one year:

The decision of a Roman tribunal, though conclusive in the particular case, had no ulterior authority except such as was given by the professional repute of the magistrate who happened to be in office for the time. Properly speaking, there was no institution at Rome during the republic analogous to the English bench.

But custom has with us greatly changed this view of Ancient Law, and precedents have acquired a vast authority. Growing, as they do, step by step, and acted upon in a thousand cases in the relations of men,— voluntarily as well as under the advice of counsel,— they naturally acquire great influence, and all the world tends to feel that they are final. Even the other co-ordinate Departments,—endowed though they are with equal authority by the instrument that created all,— are necessarily subject to this same tendency and in cases where the passions are not blazing up, and where their exercise of powers expressly conferred upon them is not concerned, are pretty certain to look to the rulings of the Courts for their guide.

The busy officer, harassed by responsibility and the opposing contentions of parties interested, is often only too glad thus to lean upon the Judiciary, and to find difficult questions solved for him. And every time that an

[16] "Ancient Law," 1st edition, pp. 34, 35.

Executive officer does in this way appeal to the rulings of the Courts and base himself upon their authority, he, of course, aids in the growth of Judicial Authority and even the establishment of their Supremacy. Man lives by custom and quickly falls into ruts.

But, at the same time, nearly all through our history, there has been a series of instances in which the Executive (the Legislature less frequently) has declined to accept the opinion of their sister department as conclusive and as binding upon them. These have generally, but not always, been cases in which the final step in the procedure in hand was to be taken by the Executive; and the question could not then, in the ordinary course of affairs, be brought before the Judiciary.

If the President thinks, as Monroe did in a controversy with the Senate,[17] that he has the right under the Constitution to appoint whom he pleases to an office newly created in the army, he will of course do so, and the Judiciary cannot interfere. Monroe did so think, and wrote:

If the law imposed such restraint [limiting his choice to a certain class], it would in that case be void.

The actual controversy here was with the Senate and, though proceedings to raise the question before the Courts were impossible, the case furnishes an instance of our system of checks and counter-checks; for the Senate persistently refused to confirm the appointments, and Monroe was, hence, compelled to yield

[17] Niles's *Register*, Vol. XXII, pp. 406, 407, 411, 415, 423.

this point. But in another controversy in the same matter, turning on the question of the President's right to transfer officers from one corps to the same grade in another corps, confirmation by the Senate not being necessary, Monroe carried his point and made the transfers.

Nor was this claim of Monroe's an isolated instance in which the Executive had simply gone askew; but the like claim has been made in a number of cases by our Presidents, though not to my knowledge within fifty years, as well as by many of our leading men. Of our Presidents, in addition to Monroe, Jefferson, Madison, Jackson, Van Buren, Lincoln, and Johnson were all either engaged in such contests or asserted the view that the opinions of the Judiciary were not conclusive, and some students of the Constitution still today maintain this opinion of our earlier years.

These precedents and opinions of our leading men must be to some extent examined here, and it will be found that they not only reach back to our earliest days but are quite occasionally to be met in our history, down to at least shortly after the Civil War.[18]

Hamilton wrote in No. XLIX of the *Federalist* that frequent recurrence should be had to the people, not only to alter, when necessary, the powers of government,

[18] Many of the instances and opinions cited have already been used in my articles on "The Relation of the Judiciary to the Constitution," in *American Law Review* (March-April, 1885), Vol. XIX, pp. 175-203, and on "The Independence of the Departments of Government," in *ibid.*, Vol. XXIII, pp. 594-609.

but also whenever any one of the departments may commit encroachments on the chartered authorities of the others. The several departments being perfectly coördinate by the terms of their common commission, neither of them, it is evident, can pretend to an exclusive or superior right of settling the boundaries between their respective powers; and how are the encroachments of the stronger to be prevented, or the wrongs of the weaker to be redressed, without an appeal to the people themselves; who, as the grantors of the commission, can alone declare its true meaning, and enforce its observance?

And again in No. LI of the same treatise upon the Constitution, Hamilton wrote upon the general subject as follows:

To what expedient then shall we finally resort, for maintaining in practice the necessary partition of power among the several departments, as laid down in the constitution? The only answer that can be given is, that as all these exterior provisions are found to be inadequate, the defect must be supplied, by so contriving the exterior structure of the government, as that its several constituent parts, may, by their mutual relations, be the means of keeping each other in their proper places. . . .

But the great security against a gradual concentration of the several powers in the same department, consists in giving to those who administer each department, the necessary constitutional means, and personal motives, to resist encroachments of the others. The provision for defense must in this as in all other cases, be made commensurate to the danger of attack. Ambition must be made to counteract ambition. The interest of the man must be connected with the constitutional rights of the place. . . . In framing a government, which is to be administered by men over men, the great difficulty lies in this: you must first enable the government to control the governed; and in the next place, oblige it to control itself.

Madison, also, wrote at some length upon the general subject in 1834, and summed up admirably the whole truth. The entire letter follows:

DEAR SIR: Having referred to the Supreme Court of the United States as a constitutional resort in deciding questions of jurisdiction between the United States and the individual States, a few remarks may be proper, showing the 'sense and degree in which that character is more particularly ascribed to that department of the government.

As the legislative, executive, and judicial departments of the United States are coördinate, and each equally bound to support the constitution, it follows that each must, in the exercise of its functions, be guided by the text of the constitution according to its own interpretation of it; and consequently, that in the event of irreconcilable interpretations, the prevalence of the one or the other department must depend on the nature of the case, as receiving its final decision from one or the other, and passing from that decision into effect, without involving the functions of any other.

It is certainly due from the functionaries of the several departments to pay much respect to the opinions of each other; and as far as official independence and obligation will permit, to consult the means of adjusting differences and avoiding practical embarrassments growing out of them, as must be done in like cases between the coördinate branches of the legislative department.

But notwithstanding this abstract view of the coördinate and independent right of the three departments to expound the constitution, the judicial department most familiarizes itself to the public attention as the expositor, by the order of its functions in relation to the other departments; and attracts most the public confidence by the composition of the tribunal.

It is the judicial department in which questions of constitutionality, as well as of legality, generally find their ultimate discussion and operative decision; and the public deference to and confidence in the judgment of the body are peculiarly inspired by the qualities implied in its members; by the gravity and deliberation of their proceedings; and by the advantage their plurality gives them over the unity of the executive department, and their fewness over the multitudinous composition of the legislative department.

Without losing sight, therefore, of the coördinate relations of the three departments to each other, it may always be expected that the judicial bench, when happily filled, will for the reasons suggested, most engage the respect and reliance of the public as the surest expositor of the constitution, as well in questions within its cognizance concerning the boundaries between the several departments of the government as in those between the Union and its members.[19]

James Wilson, another leading man in drafting our Constitution, wrote in 1790-91 :

The independency of each power [or department of government] consists in this, that its proceedings, and the motives, views, and principles, which produce those pro-

[19] "Works" by Congress (1865), Vol. IV, p. 349.

ceedings, should be free from the remotest influence, direct or indirect, of either of the other two powers. But further than this, the independence of each power ought .not to extend. Its proceedings should be formed without restraint, but when they are once formed, they should be subject to control. . . .

We are now led to discover, that between these three great departments of government, there ought to be a mutual dependency, as well as a mutual independency. We have described their independency; let us now describe their dependency. It consists in this, that the proceedings of each, when they come forth into action and are ready to affect the whole, are liable to be examined and controlled by one or both of the others.[20]

And, as if to show beyond the shadow of a doubt the broad principle that was in his mind in penning these words, Wilson had already said in the Ratifying Convention of Pennsylvania, immediately after referring to the Judiciary's right to refuse to carry out an unconstitutional law:

In the same manner the President of the United States could shield himself and refuse to carry into effect an act that violates the constitution.[21]

There could not possibly be a clearer assertion of the doctrine, which these pages seek to maintain. Wilson applied precisely the same rule of general independence to the Executive, as that which he applied to the Judiciary. Beyond peradventure, he was of opinion that

[20] "Lectures on Law," in "Works," Vol. I, pp. 409-11.
[21] "Pennsylvania and the Federal Convention," by McMaster and Stone, pp. 304-05.

each Department had the right to interpret the Constitution for itself, when called upon to act officially, and he by no means admitted that the other Departments must accept the decisions of the Judiciary as fixing the meaning of the Constitution.

Jefferson, as is well known, instructed Madison to refuse to recognize the jurisdiction of the Supreme Court in Marbury *v.* Madison, and himself declined to obey a *subpœna duces tecum* in the Burr trial;[22] and his general opinion is well set forth in the following words: In suits before them, he wrote, the judiciary

of course decide for themselves. The constitutional validity of the law or laws again prescribing executive action, and to be administered by that branch ultimately and without appeal, the executive must decide for themselves also whether under the constitution they are valid or not.

And further on, to make still more clear his meaning that each Department has the right to adhere to and defend its construction, he adds:

It may be said that contradictory decisions may arise in such cases and produce inconvenience. This is possible and is a necessary failing in all human proceedings.[23]

Jefferson's opinion was identical with that just shown to have been Wilson's.

Chief Justice Marshall also held this view, so usual

[22] Van Buren's "Political Parties in the United States," pp. 283-86, 291-93, 304.
[23] Quoted in "Johnson's Impeachment," Vol. II, p. 163.

in the early days of our country. In his famous speech in the Senate, in the case of Thomas Nash, he contended that the case was one for Executive and not for Judicial decision, and said that he

admitted implicitly the division of powers stated by the gentleman from New York [Livingston?] and that it was the duty of each department to resist the encroachments of the others.[24]

Attorney-General Wirt in 1824 gave an opinion to the First Comptroller of the Treasury, in which much the same view was again asserted. The Commissioners under the Treaty with Spain had awarded a sum of money to one Cathcart, but certain persons claiming to be his assignees filed a bill in the Circuit Court of the United States for the District of Columbia, and obtained an injunction forbidding the Federal officials from paying over the money to any one but them. Under these circumstances, Wirt wrote:

My opinion is that the judiciary can no more arrest the executive in the execution of a law, than they can arrest the legislature itself in passing the law. . . . It is, therefore, in my opinion, essential to the government itself to assert, for the executive branch, this independent action.

But at the same time he thought there were cases, and this was one, in which the Executive would do well to respect the opinion of the Judiciary, and he accordingly recommended forbearance until the Court

[24] Quoted in 5 Wheaton, Appendix, p. 15.

should decide the question; but that the jurisdiction of the Court should not be recognized by appearing to the suit as parties.[25]

President Jackson's action is also well known. Not only did he refuse to aid in the execution of the judgment of the Supreme Court in Worcester *v.* Georgia,[26] and the judgment thus remained of no effect,—but he vetoed the bank bill of 1832, on the ground that there was no constitutional power to create a bank, despite the fact that the Supreme Court had decided that the bank about to expire and proposed to be continued was constitutional.[27] Van Buren, who became Jackson's successor as President, and who was a member of the Cabinet at this time, agreed with Jackson as to his powers, and remained of the same opinion many years later.[28]

President Buchanan's opinion is not altogether clear, though in one instance he asserted quite decidedly the views I have quoted from numbers of authorities. In his inaugural address,[29] when a decision in the Dred

[25] "Opinions of the Attorneys General," Vol. I, pp. 681-686. See also Taney's opinion in 1832 in the matter of the jewels of the Princess of Orange, *ibid.*, Vol. II, pp. 482-493 and 496-99.

[26] 6 Peters, p. 515. This seems to many a very ultra action on Jackson's part, but possibly it was partly based on the probability that to execute the decree would lead to civil war.

[27] Webster argued against the action of the President in 1832, maintaining apparently that, as the chief purpose of the law was to continue the existing bank for a further period, and as the Supreme Court had decided the existing bank to be constitutional, the President had no rightful discretion to veto, because a bank was in his opinion unconstitutional. See my article on the "Relation of the Judiciary," etc., in *American Law Review*, Vol. XIX (March-April, 1885), p. 196.

[28] Van Buren's "Political Parties," Caps. VI and VIII.

[29] Curtis's "Life," Vol. II, p. 189.

Scott case was awaited, he seems perhaps to have leaned rather strongly on the views of the Judicial Department, but this may possibly have been owing to an eager desire to see the slavery question settled, rather than to any belief in that Department's peculiar function to interpret.

At a shortly later time, when President, he took quite a different view. Congress had passed a law containing an appropriation for the completion of the Washington aqueduct, to be expended according to the plans and estimates of a certain officer (naming him), and under his superintendence. When the bill came to Buchanan for signature, he sent a special message[30] to Congress, objecting to the above features as an infringement of his rights, and announcing that he should consider the naming of the particular officer by Congress merely as a recommendation. He then signed the bill, but did not appoint the officer named by Congress to the office in question. This officer thereupon sent a memorial to the Executive, objecting to his non-appointment in accordance with the terms of the Act, and Attorney-General Black wrote an opinion upon the case.

Black was of opinion that, as commander-in-chief, it was the President's right to decide what officer should perform any particular duty, and that as supreme executive magistrate, the President had the power of appointment. In continuation he said:

Congress could not, if it would, take away from the President, or in any wise diminish the authority conferred

[30] Henry's "Messages of President Buchanan," pp. 269-71.

upon him by the Constitution. . . . Congress is vested with legislative power; the authority of the President is executive. Neither has a right to interfere with the functions of the other. Every law is to be carried out so far forth as is consistent with the Constitution, and no further. The sound part of it must be executed, and the vicious portion of it suffered to drop.[31]

Lincoln, also, of our Presidents, wrote very plainly to the same general effect in one instance, and I do not know of any opinion from him to the contrary. In his first inaugural, he expressed himself as follows, with evident reference to the Dred Scott decision:

I do not forget the position assumed by some that constitutional questions are to be decided by the Supreme Court, nor do I deny that such decisions must be binding upon the parties to that suit: while they are also entitled to very high respect and consideration in all parallel cases by all the departments of the government. . . . [But the candid citizen must confess that] if the policy of the government upon the vital questions affecting the whole people is to be irrevocably fixed by the decisions of the Supreme Court, the moment they are made, as in ordinary cases between parties in personal actions, the people will have ceased to be their own masters, having to that extent resigned their government into the hands of that eminent tribunal.

[31] "Opinions of the Attorneys General," Vol. IX, pp. 463-75. About twenty years later (1882) a precisely like provision was inserted in the Sundry Civil Bill in relation to the proposed new Pension Building, but in this instance the bill was signed without objection and the officer indicated in the act was appointed.

But the contest between Johnson and the leaders of the majority in Congress, after the Civil War, is the instance in our history in which the question we are concerned with met with the most elaborate consideration. Congress had passed a law on March 3, 1865, which was approved by Lincoln, providing that assistant assessors of internal revenue should be appointed by the assessors, and repealing all laws inconsistent therewith. Such assessors had theretofore been appointed by the Secretary of the Treasury, under the Act of June 30, 1864.

When Johnson came into office after Lincoln's death, he evidently wanted to make these appointments, but the Act of March 3, 1865, seemed to stand in the way. Attorney-General Speed thereupon gave it as his opinion that the attempt by that statute to vest the appointment in the assessors was clearly unconstitutional, and that as the former method of appointment by the Secretary of the Treasury, under the Act of June 30, 1864, was repealed by the Act of 1865, there was no statute in effect providing a method for their appointment. Speed was of opinion that the assistant assessors were "officers," within the meaning of clause 2, section 2 of Article II of the Constitution, and that the right of appointing them hence devolved upon the President. He adds that the right should be exercised by him, despite the fact that by the Act of 1865 Congress had distinctly declared their will to be that he should not appoint the assistant assessors.

It is to be noted, however, that the course of action

advised by Speed was apparently intended by him to
lead up to a judicial decision of the question, in a contest between an appointee of the President and one
appointed by the assessor under the provisions of the
Act of 1865. It seems, therefore, that while Speed
did not hold that the President must slavishly enforce
all statutes on the book, he yet took a view of the chief
question far removed from that hereinbefore quoted
from a number of earlier authorities.

As the partisan contest between Johnson and the
leaders opposed to him went on, the quarrel grew more
and more bitter, until at length, after Johnson had
refused to obey some of the utterly unjustifiable and
even revolutionary statutes driven through Congress
over his veto by the majority leaders, still flaming with
the passions of the Civil War and absolutely determined to rule, they brought into the House articles of
impeachment against him. The chief issues involved in
the trial before the Senate grew out of laws which
Johnson held to have infringed his constitutional right
to command the army and his right to remove from
office.

The constitutional right of the President to adhere
to his understanding of the language of the Constitution, and to necessary inference therefrom in regard
to his powers, and to refuse to obey a statute taking
such powers from him, was the subject of wide discussion; and the right to refuse to obey was claimed
for him, in a greater or less degree, by every one of
his counsel and by several of the Senators who voted

for acquittal.[32] Again here, as in the case of Speed's opinion, much was said by counsel and others, of the refusal to obey being a step leading up to a judicial decision; but it may probably be supposed that this grew largely out of the tact of the advocate who does not want in matters of difficulty to claim more than the needs of his case require. Johnson had, moreover, throughout the contest maintained that his course was based on that idea.

It was during the same memorable quarrel between Congress and President Johnson that Gideon Welles had a conversation with Grant, who had recently been appointed Secretary of War, which is noteworthy and may even show how the ancient belief was possibly at that time being substituted by the new. Welles spoke of the differences between Congress and the President, and records that he was pained to see how little Grant knew of the Constitution and our Government. Grant said of the "Reconstruction" law that Congress had enacted it, and the President must execute it. "If the law was unconstitutional," he said, "the judges alone could decide the question. The President must submit and obey Congress until the Supreme Court set the law aside." I asked him, so

[32] See, in the volumes of the Impeachment Trial, the arguments of Curtis, Vol. I, pp. 386-88; Nelson, Vol. II, pp. 160-68; Groesbeck, Vol. II, pp. 198-200; Evarts, Vol. II, pp. 292-97, 320-21; Stanbery, Vol. II, pp. 373-76, 382-83; and the opinions of Buckalew, Vol. III, p. 232; Doolittle, *ibid.*, p. 246; Henderson, *ibid.*, pp. 303-04; Grimes, *ibid.*, pp. 337-38; Johnson, *ibid.*, pp. 55-57; Vickers, *ibid.*, p. 117; Davis, *ibid.*, p. 170, 172-73, 176-77; Fowler, *ibid.*, p. 207. Sumner and Patterson, also, admitted the President's right to refuse to execute laws palpably violating the Constitution; *ibid.*, pp. 273 and 312.

Welles goes on, if Congress could exercise powers not granted, powers expressly reserved to the States, which made the Constitution. Grant replied that "Congress might pass any law, and the President and all others must obey and support it until the Supreme Court declared it unconstitutional."[33]

A few theoretical writers,—who have studied the question under the diffused light coming from all sources, and in its manifold relations,—may also be cited here. Still more holding distinctly the same view could be found, and at the same time many others, who hold much the same confused opinions which Welles gives us from a great soldier. Bancroft, who had studied our history from its beginnings, and had written on the Constitution itself, evidently by no means accepted the belief in Judicial Finality. Towards the end of his long life, he wrote:

The decision of that court in all cases within its jurisdiction is final between the parties to the suit and must be carried into effect by the proper officers; but, as an interpretation of the constitution, it does not bind the President or the Legislature of the United States. . . . [After referring to the fact that the irreversibility of their decisions attaches only to the parties to the suit, and that society submits in order to escape from daily anarchy] : To the decision of an underlying question of constitutional law, no such finality attaches. To endure it must be right. If it is right, it will approve itself to

[33] "The Diary of Gideon Welles," Vol. III, pp. 176-180, cited in Andrew C. McLaughlin's "The Courts, The Constitution, and the People," pp. 59-60.

the universal sense of the impartial. . . . An act of the Legislature at variance with the constitution is pronounced void; an opinion of the Supreme Court at variance with the constitution is equally so.[34]

Professor Thayer, too, of Harvard, wrote, in words that sum up clearly enough the reason for the origin of our Courts' action, yet at the same time words that do not at all recognize their conclusive effect on all the world:

Again, where the power of the judiciary did have place, its whole scope was this; namely, to determine, for the mere purpose of deciding a litigated question properly submitted to the court, whether a particular disputed exercise of power was forbidden by the constitution.[35]

Finally, Professor McLaughlin, of the University of Chicago, writing as late as 1912, by no means accepts the doctrine of Judicial Supremacy. On the contrary, he is of opinion that the Courts have no special powers in the matter, and are "only exercising their freedom within their own province" when they hold a law unconstitutional. At the same time, he writes:

Possibly American constitutional law has grown away from its early conditions; the principle of separation and of judicial independence, not judicial superiority, was beyond question distinctly put forth by the judges in the early cases, and on that basis the courts did, as a his-

[34] "History of the Constitution," Vol. II, pp. 198, 202, 203.
[35] "American Doctrine of Constitutional Law," in *Harvard Law Review*, Vol. VII, p. 9.

torical fact, act and assume authority to deny the validity of legislation.[36]

And he recognizes fully the view that these pages have shown was held by so many of our earlier leaders, and even the right of the President to refuse to be bound by an unconstitutional Act of Congress.[37]

From all that precedes, it is amply apparent that Judicial Supremacy had no place in the beliefs of the Founders and of their successors, for a number of years. The Judiciary was at that time far too weak to make such a claim, and would merely have brought ridicule on itself by so doing. Nor did any one else, so far as I know, make the claim on their behalf. Indeed, they felt most strongly the need of showing some foundation for their mere action in declining to enforce a statute, and they largely found their justification in insisting that, under our written Constitutions, they were a coördinate Department.

What was to be the indirect result of their action in a long course of years they did not discuss and probably did not consider. Men rarely do look far ahead, for the simple reason that, owing to their limitations, they cannot do so. The Courts in those early cases merely decided that, as they were one of the great coördinate branches of Government, with functions as clearly set forth by the written Constitution as were those of the Legislature or the Executive, they must

[36] Andrew C. McLaughlin's "The Courts, The Constitution, and The People," pp. 62 et seq. See Chapter III generally for the history of the matter and the author's general opinion.
[37] Ibid., p. 62, footnote.

exercise the powers confided to them, and could not be called upon, against their clear convictions, to aid in carrying out a law of Congress which they held to be a plain violation of the fundamental instrument. They would probably have equally conceded the same right to the other Departments, when these were in turn called upon to assist the Judiciary. Such was, at least, the necessary result of their arguments to justify their own action.

That all this has perhaps been immensely changed in the years that have elapsed since our beginnings, is too plain for discussion, let alone for doubt. Possibly our historical growth in the matter has gone so far as to justify the use of the term "Judicial Supremacy." Some think so, and not a few would probably even accept the opinions which Grant expressed to Welles. But constitutional doctrines deriving their origin in such a manner, by very slow growth against a view generally accepted at an earlier date, and against what seems surely to be the true theory of the matter, are always nebulous for many, many years,[38] and may even be rejected at a very late date.

In relation, then, to the question of what is the true doctrine of Judicial Power in our country, there is

---

[38] As late as 1851 Disraeli thought that the veto of the Crown had not lapsed by disuse, but that an occasion might arise "when, supported by the sympathies of a loyal people, its exercise might defeat an unconstitutional Ministry and a corrupt Parliament." "Life," by Monypenny and Buckle, Vol. III, p. 321. The question, too, of the circumstances under which the Lords were constitutionally obliged to yield to the insistence of the Commons upon a special measure, though it was widely asserted that there was such an obligation, was never settled until the statute of a few years ago.

certainly still the gravest doubt. Many hold that the decrees of the Judiciary are absolutely final, and must be accepted by all,—Departments of Government, as well as individuals; but not a few writers are still to be found, who deny any such conclusion, and in a number of instances, down to within about half a century, leading officials have spoken and even officially acted against it. And very recently quite a school has sprung up, which denies not only Supremacy to Judicial decisions, but denies even their right to hold any law unconstitutional,—at least, any law passed by Congress.

It still remains to the future to show whether gradual historical growth has established the doctrine of Judicial Supremacy in our country, or whether, with the immensely grown power of our Executive, and perhaps under the inducements of the terrible death-struggle now prevailing throughout the world, the older doctrine will not yet crop up again, and the essential weakness of the Judiciary result in a complete denial to them of any Supremacy, or even the occasional refusal to allow the enforcement of specific decrees entered by them.

INDEX

Adams, John, 49, 52, 56, 193, 196.
Adams, Sam, quoted, 166.
Adams's "Gallatin," cited, 213.
Alien and Sedition Acts, 219.
"American Colonial Government," Oliver Morton Dickerson, cited, 20, 23, 26, 104.
American Doctrine, The, 9 *et seq.*, 46, 134 *et seq.*
"American Doctrine, The." *See* Thayer.
"American Doctrine of Judicial Supremacy, The," Charles Grove Haines, cited, 35, 46, 208.
American Historical Review, 40, 60, 61, 135, 174, 179, footnotes.
"American Judiciary, The." *See* Baldwin.
American Law Review, 7, 8, 12, 60, 75, 174, 194, 223, 230, footnotes.
American Political Science Review, 12, 74, 128, 148, footnotes.
American Quarterly Review, 194, 218, footnotes.
"American State papers, Misc.," cited, 178.
"Annulment of Legislation." *See* Horace A. Davis.
"A Phantom Precedent," cited, 60.

"Appeals from Colonial Courts to the King in Council" etc., Harold D. Hazeltine, 24, footnote.
Appleton's Dictionary, cited, 72.
Argentina, 12.
Aristides. *See* Hanson.
Ashe, Judge, 113.
Aurora, quoted, 182, 216.
Austin *v.* Trustees, 176.
Australia, 12.

Bacon's "Abridgment," 57.
Bahamas, 22.
Baldwin, Simeon E., cited, 168, 185, 203; quoted, 209.
Bancroft, George, quoted, 236, 237.
Bank of the United States, 173.
Bassett, 136, 171.
Batchellor, Albert S., 75, footnote.
Battle's "Address on the History of the Supreme Court," cited, 114, 120, 217.
Bayard *v.* Singleton, 101-123, 129, 133, 176.
Beard, Professor, 148, footnote.
Beatty, Major, 77.
Benson, Egbert, 86.
Benton's "Abridgment," cited, 194, 219.
Bidwell, 68.
Bismark, 207.